AgiliWriting ®
The Readable Shorthand
of the English Language

by
Anne Gresham

Agilityping Ltd

First published in Great Britain in 1990 by
© **AGILITYPING LTD**
London, England

Second Printing 1992

Copyright © **Anne Gresham 1986**

WORLD RIGHTS RESERVED

AgiliWriting ® and **AgiliTyping** ®
are the registered trademarks of Agilityping Ltd.

IBM ® **IBM PC** ® are the registered trademarks of IBM Corporation.
Wordstar ® is the registered trademark of Wordstar International.

British Library Cataloguing in Publication Data
Gresham, Anne
    AgiliWriting : the readable shorthand of the English language.
    1. Shorthand
    1. Title
    653

ISBN 1-87296-800-7

Typeset by:
Justa Mo, Cheshunt, Herts

Cartoons by:
Allin Kempthorne-Ley-Edwards, London

Cover by:
Design 29, Dyfed

Printed in Great Britain by:
Loader Jackson Printers, Arlesey, Bedfordshire.

CONTENTS

AgiliWriting Dictionary of Abbreviated Words
is an accompaniment to this book.

Acknowledgement:

My sincere thanks for the encouragement and support given to me by my daughters, and Beryl, Jeremy, and Simon.

FOREWORD

AgiliWriting shorthand has been created so that the English language can be written quickly in an abbreviated readable form wherever the writing of it is a major activity in private or business life. Its phonetic principles are easily learnt, spelling is irrelevant, and only standard letters of the English alphabet are used.

AgiliWriting shorthnd hzbn crytd so tht th Nglsh lngwj cnb wrtn qkly n an abrvytd rdbl fm, wrvr th wrtg v it s a majr actvty n prvt or bznz lyf. Its fnetc prnzpls r ezly lrnt, spelg s irlvnt, nd only stndrd ltrs v th Nglsh alfbt r uzd.

Anne Gresham, a teacher of the English language, developed **AgiliWriting** following many years of careful study of the English language to provide a rapidly assimilated shorthand which is easy to learn, easy to write, and, moreover, easy to sight-read even by untrained **AgiliWriters**.

AgiliTyping software
For those who use an IBM compatible computer, the **AgiliWriting** system of shorthand offers the additional advantage of the complementary software, **AgiliTyping**, which automatically transcribes **AgiliWriting** shorthand text into full English.

Refer to end of book.

Refer to end of book.

INTRODUCTION

SUMMARY OF PRINCIPLES

The **Agiliwriting** system of shorthand has been designed so that it can be easily read in its abbreviated form. The **Agiliwriting** principles of abbreviation are outlined in this section.

Writing by Sound

AGILIWRITING shorthand is based on **phonetics**. This means that as far as possible, words are written according to their **spoken sound.**

In ordinary spelling, many words contain letters which are phonetically weak or silent; these letters contribute little or nothing to the **SOUND** of the word.

AGILIWRITING abbreviates words by substituting or eliminating these auxiliary letters.

Examples:

In the word **'spell'**, one of the pair of **double letters** is **phonetically silent** and may be deleted without affecting the readability of the word.

spell = spel

In the word **'vote'**, the silent letter **'e'** may be deleted without affecting the readability of the word.

vote = vot

The word **'be'** SOUNDS identical to the single letter **'b'**; the letter **'e'** is deleted and **'be'** becomes **'b'**.

be = b

The word **'are'** SOUNDS identical to the single letter **'r'**; the letters **'a'** and **'e'** are deleted and **'are'** becomes **'r'**.

are = r

The word **'you'** SOUNDS identical to the single letter **'u'**. The letters **'y'** and **'o'** are deleted and the word **'you'** becomes **'u'**.

you = u

'SHORT-HARD and LONG-SOFT SOUNDS

There are **26** letters in the English alphabet. Five of these are called **'vowels'** - **a,e,i,o,u.** The rest of the letters are called **'consonants'**.

The variation in the **SOUNDS** conveyed by the **vowels** and **consonants** in different combinations can be likened to a musical composition; in some combinations a **'short-hard'** sound will be produced and in other combinations, a **'long-soft'** sound will be produced.

VOWELS

The underlined vowels **a,e,i,o,u,** in row (1) produce a **'SHORT-HARD'** sound. The underlined vowels **a,e,i,o,u,** in row (2) produce a **'LONG-SOFT'** sound:

    (1) RAT BED BIT BOND RUG   'short-hard'
    (2) RAte BE BITe BONe RULe   'long-soft'

CONSONANTS

The consonants **'c'** and **'g'** in row (1) produce a **'SHORT-HARD'** sound:
The consonants **'c'** and **'g'** in row (2) produce a **'LONG-SOFT'** sound:

    (1) Car   Gun   daGGer   **'short-hard'**
    (2) Centre   Germ   saGe   **'long-soft'**

The **'short-hard'** consonants **'c'** and **'g'** do not change.

car = **car**

gun = **gun**

dagger* = **dagr**

*ger = gr
*Double letter become single letters

The **'long-soft'** consonant **'c'** with which words such as **'centre'** and **'certain'** begin, changes to **'s'**:

centre = **sntr**

(**en = n**, silent vowel 'e' is deleted)

certain = **srtn**

(**er = r**, 'tain = **tn'**)

The **'long-soft'** consonant **'g'** in the words - **'sage'** and **'germ'** changes to **'j'.**

sage = sa**j**

(silent vowel **'e'** is deleted)

germ = **j**rm

(er = r)

LINKED CONSONANTS

There are consonants which are linked together to produce only **one sound.** For example, the **linked consonants 'dg'** in the words - **'bridge'** and **'wedge',** etc., produce the **single sound 'j'.** These linked consonants are replaced by the single consonant **'j'.**

bridge = **brij**

wedge = **wej**

(silent vowel 'e' is deleted)

The **linked consonants 'ck' in the words - 'clock',** and **'tackle'** etc. are replaced by the single consonant **'k'.**

clock = **clok**

tackle = **takl***

*Silent vowel **'e'** is deleted

VOWELS

'SHORT-HARD' and 'LONG-SOFT' SOUNDS

The vowel 'i'.

The vowel 'i' has two sounds

The **'short-hard'** sound as in the words - **bit, fit, lid;** the vowel **'i'** remains as **'i'**.

$$bit = \mathbf{bit}$$
$$fit = \mathbf{fit}$$
$$lid = \mathbf{lid}$$

The **'long-soft'** sound of 'i' as in the words - **bite, fight** and **lied;** the vowel **'i'** is replaced by **'y'; silent vowels and consonants are deleted:**

$$bite = \mathbf{byt}$$
$$fight = \mathbf{fyt}$$
$$lied = \mathbf{lyd}$$

i)   The silent vowel **'e'** terminating the word **'bite'** is deleted.
ii)   The silent consonants **'gh'** in the word **'fight'** are deleted.
iii)   The linked vowels **'ie'** in the word **'lied'** produce the single sound **'i';** the silent vowel **'e'** is deleted.

The vowel **'u'**.

The vowel **'u'** has two sounds.
The **'short-hard'** sound as in the words - **bug, cub,** and **tub;** the **'short-hard'** sound remains as **'u'**.

$$bug = \mathbf{bug}$$
$$cub = \mathbf{cub}$$
$$tub = \mathbf{tub}$$

The **'long-soft'** sound of **'u'** as in the words **'bugle'**, **'cubic'** and **'tube'**; the vowel **'u'** is replaced by **'w'**.

$$bugle = \mathbf{bwgl}$$
$$cubic = \mathbf{cwbc}$$
$$tube = \mathbf{twb}$$

All other vowels are deleted, as the vowel **'u'** is the highest vowel in the **Agiliwriting** phonetic scale applicable to the vowels. (See chapter 'Deletion of the Vowels').

COMMON SOUNDS

In ordinary longhand, words or syllables which **SOUND** the same are spelt differently, but as **Agiliwriting** is a **PHONETIC** shorthand, syllables or combinations of letters which **SOUND** alike are given similar abbreviations.

1. The **common sounds** in the following examples are - **'cent'**, **'scent'**, and **'sent'**. These are abbreviated to **'snt'**.

Double letters become **single** letters.
Silent vowels and consonants are eliminated.

Word	*Syllables*	*Agiliwriting*
accent	ac/**cent**	**acsnt**
assent	as/**sent**	**asnt**
descent	de/**scent**	**dsnt**
percent	per/**cent**	**prsnt**
sent	**sent**	**snt**

2. The **common sounds** in the following examples are - 'scer', 'cer', 'cir', 'ser', 'sir', 'swer'. These are abbreviated to 'sr'.

Word	Syllables	Agiliwriting
ascertain	a/**scer**/tain	**asrtn***
certain	**cer**/tain	**srtn***
circle	**cir**/cle	**srcl**
serve	**serve**	**srv**
sir	**sir**	**sr**
answer	an/**swer**	**ansr**

*'tain = **tn**'

3. The following **one-syllable** words contain combinations having **common sounds** but **different spellings;** these combinations are given similar abbreviations:

Word	Syllables	Agiliwriting
birch	bir = **br**	**brch**
burn	bur = **br**	**brn**
dirt	dir = **dr**	**drt**
dearth	dear = **dr**	**drth**
her	her = **hr**	**hr**
hurt	hur = **hr**	**hrt**
perch	per = **pr**	**prch**
search	sear = **sr**	**srch**

THE PRINCIPLES OF ABBREVIATION

The **Agiliwriting** rules for abbreviating words in the English language are based on three main principles:

1) Abbreviation of the **ROOT WORD** - the **trunk of the tree**
2) Abbreviation of **PREFIXES & SUFFIXES** - the **branches of the tree**
3) **DELETION OF THE VOWELS** - the **foliage springing from these branches**

1) Abbreviation of ROOT WORD

ROOT WORD: **SERVE = SRV**
(**ser = sr,** silent vowel **'e'** is deleted)

ROOT WORD: **TEND = TND**
(en = n)

ROOT WORD: **VOTE = VOT**
(silent vowel 'e' is deleted)

2) Abbreviation of PREFIXES & SUFFIXES

i) In the word **con/SERV/ing**
  'con' = prefix   **'cn'** = abbreviation of prefix
  'ing' = suffix   **'g'** = abbreviation of suffix
  CONSERVING = cn/SRV/g = CNSRVG

ii) In the word **ex/TEND/ing**
  'ex' = prefix   **'x'** = abbreviation of prefix
  'ing' = suffix   **'g'** = abbreviation of suffix
  EXTENDING = x/TND/g = XTNDG

iii) In the word **de/VOT/ing**
  'de' = prefix   **'d'** = abbreviation of prefix
  'ing' = suffix   **'g'** = abbreviation of suffix
  DEVOTING = d/VOT/g = DVOTG

3) DELETION OF THE VOWELS

Agiliwriting utilises a **phonetic scale** which applies to the **vowels**. This scale adopts the ascending order: **e,i,a,o,u.**

The vowel **'e'** is considered to be the least phonetically resonant and lies at the bottom of the scale. The vowel **'u'** is considered to be the most phonetically resonant and lies at the top of the scale.

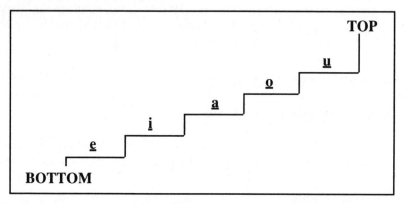

i) Where words contain more than one vowel, the vowels are deleted according to their position in the phonetic scale. **Only the highest vowel in the phonetic scale is retained; all the other lower vowels are deleted.**

Word	*Highest Vowel*	*Agiliwriting*
cultivate	u	**cultvt**
understand	u	**undrstnd**
tolerant	o	**tolrnt**
order	o	**ordr**
dismantle	a	**dsmantl**
ability	a	**ablty**
shiver	i	**shivr**
idle	i	**idl**

ii) Where the **commencing vowel** is lower in the phonetic scale than the highest vowel contained in a word, both the **commencing** vowel and the **highest** vowel are retained.

Word	Highest Vowel	Agiliwriting
electronic	o	elctronc
evade	a	evad

The principles of **Agiliwriting** are fully explained in the following chapters, commencing with a **'Quick Learning Guide'** which should enable the reader to utilise the principles of **Agiliwriting** within a few hours.

The **Agiliwriting** system of shorthand as presented in this **'teach-yourself'** book has been constructed so that the English language can be written quickly in a readable form whilst retaining the Roman alphabet.

Its use can be extended on a computer by means of the **Agilityping software*** which automatically translates the shorthand text into full standard English form.
(* Refer to back of book.)

Principles of Abbreviation

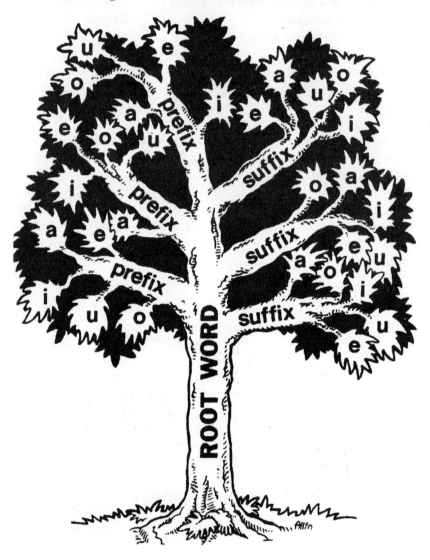

Agiliwriting Shorthand

CHAPTER 1

QUICK LEARNING GUIDE

The **Agiliwriting** rules for abbreviating words are based on three main principles:

(1)   Abbreviation of **ROOT WORD** - the **trunk of the tree**.
(2)   Abbreviation of **PREFIXES & SUFFIXES** - the **branches of the tree**.
(3)   Deletion of the **VOWELS** - the **foliage springing from these branches**.

(1)   Abbreviation of the **ROOT WORD**

Root Word	*Agiliwriting*	
serve	**srv***	(er = **r**)
tend	**tnd**	(en = **n**)
vote	**vot***	

*Silent vowel 'e' is deleted.

(2) Abbreviation of **PREFIXES & SUFFIXES**

    i) In the word - **con/SERV/ing**

        'con'= PREFIX   **'cn'**= abbreviation of PREFIX
        'ing'= SUFFIX   **'g'** = abbreviation of SUFFIX

    CONSERVING = cn/SRV/g = **CNSRVG**

    ii) In the word - **ex/TEND/ing**

        'ex'= PREFIX   **'x'** = abbreviation of PREFIX
        'ing'= SUFFIX   **'g'** = abbreviation of SUFFIX

    EXTENDING = x/TND/g = **XTNDG**

    iii) In the word - **de/VOT/ing**

        'de'= PREFIX   **'d'** = abbreviation of PREFIX
        'ing'= SUFFIX   **'g'**= abbreviation of SUFFIX

    DEVOTING = d/VOT/g = **DVOTG**

(3) DELETION OF THE VOWELS

The vowels take the order of a **'phonetic scale'** similar to a musical scale. This scale is - **e,i,a,o,u.**

The vowel **'e'** lies at the **bottom** of the scale and is considered to be the **least** phonetically resonant.

The vowel **'u'** lies at the **top** of the scale and is considered to be the **most** phonetically resonant.

The vowels are **deleted** in accordance with this phonetic scale; only the **highest** vowel being retained.

A **mnemonic** may help in remembering the vowel order.

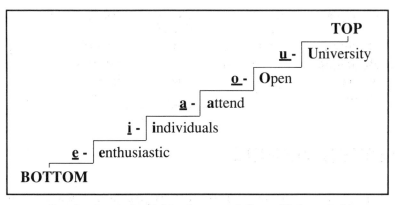

('enthusiastic individuals attend Open University')

i)   Where more than one vowel occurs in a word, the vowel which is **highest** in the scale is retained; **all the remaining lower vowels are deleted**:

Word	Syllables	Highest Vowel	Agiliwriting
multiple	mul/ti/ple	u	**multpl**
renovate	ren/o/vate	o	**rnovt**
dismantle	dis/man/tle	a	**dsmantl**
filter	fil/ter	i	**filtr**

ii)   Where a word commences with a vowel higher in the scale than the other vowel(s) occurring in the word; only the commencing vowel is retained; **all the remaining lower vowels are deleted:**

Word	Syllables	Highest Vowel	Agiliwriting
understand	un/der/stand	u	undrstnd
obstacle	ob/sta/cle	o	obstcl
able	a/ble	a	abl
item	i/tem	i	itm

iii) Where a word **commences** with a vowel **lower** in the scale than the highest vowel occurring in the word; **both the commencing vowel and the highest vowel are retained;** any remaining vowels are deleted.

Word	Syllables	Highest Vowel	Agiliwriting
abundant	a/bun/dant	u	abundnt
electronic	e/lec/tro/nic	o	elctronc
ignore	ig/nore	o	ignor
evade	e/vade	a	evad

REPEATED VOWELS

i)   Where a vowel other than 'o' or 'u' is **repeated** in a word, it is **deleted throughout.**

Examples:

Word	Syllables	Repeated Vowel	Agiliwriting
between	be/tween	e	btwn
finish	fi/nish	i	fnsh
standard	stan/dard	a	stndrd

ii)   Where a word **commences** with a vowel and the vowel is **repeated** in the
      word, **only the commencing vowel is retained.**

Word	Syllables	Repeated Vowel	Agiliwriting
eleven	e/le/ven	e	**elvn**
immit	im/mit	i	**imt***
attach	at/tach	a	**atch***

*No double letters

THE VOWELS 'o' and 'u'

iii) Where the vowel **'o'** is repeated in a word, the vowel **'o'** in the first syllable
      is retained unless the word contains either of the abbreviations **'com=cm'**,
      or **'con = cn'**.

Examples:

Word	Syllables	Agiliwriting
cotton	cot/ton	**cotn***
doctor	doc/tor	**doctr**
motor	mo/tor	**motr**

*No double letters

Word	Syllables	Agiliwriting
commodity	com/mo/dity	**cmodty***
concoct	con/coct	**cncoct**
economic	e/con/o/mic	**ecnomc**

*No double letters

iv)   Where the vowel **'u'** is repeated in a word, the vowel **'u'** in the first
      syllable of the word is retained.

Examples:

Word	Syllables	Agiliwriting
cultural	cul/tu/ral	**cultrl**
luxury	lux/ury	**luxry**
structure	struc/ture	**structr**

LINKED VOWELS

These are vowels which are **linked together** to produce only **one sound**; for example, 'oa' as in the word **'broad'** and **'ou'** as in the words **'mount'**.

'Linked Vowels' such as - *'oa', 'ou', 'au', 'ui', 'ou'*, etc. are represented by **'w'**.

Examples:

Word	Linked Vowels	Agiliwriting
abroad	oa = w	abrwd
count	ou = w	cwnt
faulty	au = w	fwlty
fruit	ui = w	frwt
look	oo = w	lwk

The combinations - **'augh'** and **'ough'** as in the words **'caught'** and **'bought'** are represented by **'aw'**.

Examples:

Word	Combinations	Agiliwriting
bought	ough = aw	bawt
fought	ough = aw	fawt
caught	augh = aw	cawt
naughty	augh = aw	nawty

DIPTHONGS

These are vowels which are **'linked together'** to produce **two sounds**; for example - 'ea' as in the word **'permeate'**, and - **'ue'** as in the word **'fluent'**.

1) Where the first vowel in a **'dipthong'** is - **'e'** or **'i'**, as in - *'ia', 'iu', 'io', 'ea', 'ie'*, etc., these 'dipthong vowels' are replaced by **'y'**;

Any remaining vowels are deleted with the exception of the **commencing vowel** and the vowels **'o'** or **'u'**.

Examples:-

Word	Dipthong	Agiliwriting
jovial	ia = y	jovyl
medium	iu = y	mdym
onion	io = y	onyn
permeate	ea = y	prmyt
proprietor	ie = y	proprytr

2) Where the first vowel in a **'dipthong'** is **'o'** or **'u'** as in - *'ua'*, *'ue'*, *'oe'*, *'ui'*, etc., these 'dipthong vowels' are replaced by - **'w'**.

Any remaining vowels are deleted with the exception of the commencing vowel and the vowels **'o'** or **'u'**.

Examples:

Word	Dipthong	Agiliwriting
fluctuate	ua = w	fluctwt
fluent	ue = w	flwnt
poetry	oe = w	pwtry
ruin	ui = w	rwn

THE VOWEL 'I'

The phonetics applicable to the **vowel 'i'**.

The vowel **'i'** has two distinctly different sounds - the **short-hard** sound of **'i'** as in the word **'bit'** and the **long-soft** sound of **'i'** as in the word **'bite'**.

1) Words containing the **short-hard** sound of **'i'** - the **'i'** remains unchanged.

2) Words containing the **long-soft** sound of **'i'** - the **'i'** is replaced by **'y'**; any remaining vowels are deleted.

short- hard sound	long-soft sound
bit = bit	bite = **byt**
rid = rid	ride = **ryd**
win = win	wine = **wyn**

2)   In words commencing with **'i', the 'i'** remains unchanged:-

ill* = **il**

item = **itm**

idle = **idl**

*No double letters

*The vowel **'i'** is the highest vowel in the above examples, the lower vowel **'e' is deleted.**

3)   Where words contain the **long-soft** sound of **'i', linked to a silent vowel and/or silent consonant(s),** as in the combinations - **'eigh', 'ie', 'igh', 'ui'**, the combinations are represented by **'y'**:

Word	*Combination*	*Agiliwriting*
height	**eigh** = y	**hyt**
right	**igh** = y	**ryt**
tie	**ie** = y	**ty**
guide	**ui** = y	**gyd***

*Silent vowel **'e' is deleted.**

From the above examples it can be seen that words are abbreviated according to their **SOUND,** i.e. **silent vowels and consonants are deleted.**

THE VOWEL 'U'

The phonetics applicable to the **vowel 'u'.**

The vowel **'u'** has two distinctly different sounds - the **short-hard** sound of **'u'** as in the word 'tub' and the **long-soft** sound of **'u'** as in the word **'tube'.**

1)   In words containing the **'short-hard'** sound of **'u'**- the **'u'** remains unchanged.

2)   In words containing the **'long-soft'** sound of **'u'** - the **'u'** is represented by **'w'**.

Examples:

short- hard sound	long-soft sound
u = u	u = w
bundle = **bundl***	bugle = **bwgl***
cut = **cut**	acute = **acwt***
tub = **tub**	tube = **twb***

*Silent vowel 'e' is deleted.

*Remember that 'u' is the highest vowel in the 'phonetic scale'. All other vowels are deleted.

SHORTS

SHORTS are frequently used words which are reasily recognisable in their abbreviated form and can be as short as one character.

Words in this category have to be memorised as they do not conform to the **Agiliwriting** rules applicable to the deletion of the vowels since apart from the commencing vowel, they contain **consonants* only.**

Examples:

Word	*Agiliwriting*
are	**r**
be	**b**
bank	**bnk**
can	**cn**
customer	**cstmr**
is	**s**
market	**mrkt**
of	**v**
possible	**psbl**
shall	**shl**
to	**t**
they	**thy**
will	**wl**
would	**wd**
your	**y**

Exceptions
our = **ur**, you = **u**

The following sentence is made up of words which come under the category of
SHORTS:

> **W r plsd t nfm u tht w hv tdy snt t u th bxs v slvr rngs u rqr. W cn azr
> u tht u wl fnd thm vry gd slrs n y knd v mrkt. W hp it wl b psbl f u t
> cm t Lndn ths szn t z th lrj nmbr v gds n ur shwrm.**

*We are pleased to inform you that we have today sent to you the boxes of
silver rings you require. We can assure you that you will find them very
good sellers in your kind of market. We hope it will be possible for you to
come to London this season to see the large number of goods in our
showroom.*

STRINGS

STRINGS further abbreviate the basic shorthand by **stringing together words**
in commonly used phrases for **speed purposes.**

Example 1.

In reply to your enquiry of
N rply t y   nqry   v   BASIC SHORTHAND
N rp   t y   nq   v
Nrptynqv   STRING

Example 2.

In reply to your letter of
N rp   t y   ltr   v   BASIC SHORTHAND
N rp   t y   l   v
Nrptylv   STRING

Example 3.

In reply to your quotation of
N rply t y   qwtn   v   BASIC SHORTHAND
N rp   t y   qt   v
Nrptyqtv   STRING

Example 4.

We are in receipt of your letter of
W r n rzt   v y   ltr   v   BASIC SHORTHAND
W r n r   v y   l   v
Wrnrvylv   **STRING**

Example 5.

We are pleased to inform you
W r plsd   t nfm   u   BASIC SHORTHAND
W r pl   t nfm   u
Wrpltnfmu   **STRING**

Example 6.

At your earliest convenience
At y   erlyst cnvnynz   BASIC SHORTHAND
at y   erl   cnv
Atyerlcnv   **STRING**

CHAPTER 2

Allin   *HAVING A GO*

ROOT WORDS

EXTENDING ROOT WORDS:

i)   A **ROOT WORD is the 'trunk of the tree'.** The form of the **'root word'** does not change with the application of a **prefix and/or suffix - 'the branches of the tree'.**

ii)   A **ROOT WORD** can hold **consonants only, or consonants and one vowel.** *Only the vowel in the ROOT WORD is retained.

Exercise 1.

Extend the abbreviated **'root word'** by applying the abbreviated **prefixes** and **suffix:**

ROOT WORD: SERVE = SRV
             (er = r, silent vowel 'e' is deleted)

Prefixes: - 'con = cn', 'de = d', 're = r'.
Suffix: - 'ing = g'

                            SERV/**ing**
             con/SERVE,   con/SERV/**ing**
             de/SERVE,   de/SERV/**ing**
             re/SERVE,   re/SERV/**ing**

Exercise 2.

Extend the abbreviated **'root word'** by applying the abbreviated **prefixes** and **suffix:**

ROOT WORD: **TEND = TND** (en = **n**)

Prefixes: 'con = **cn**', 'dis = **ds**', 'ex = **x**', 'in = **n**'
Suffix: 'ing = **g**'

TEND/**ing**

con/TEND,	**con**/TEND/**ing**
dis/TEND,	**dis**/TEND/**ing**
ex/TEND,	**ex**/TEND/**ing**
in/TEND,	**in**/TEND/**ing**

Exercise 3.

Extend the abbreviation of the **'root word'** by applying the abbreviated **prefix** and **suffix:**

ROOT WORD: VOTE = VOT
              (silent vowel **'e'** is deleted)

Prefix: - 'de = **d**'
Suffix: - **ing = g**'

VOT/**ing**

de/VOTE,   **de**/VOT/**ing**

DELETION OF THE VOWELS

The **'phonetic scale'** applicable to the deletion of the vowels is given below. (A **mnemonic** is given to assist in the remembering of the vowel order.)

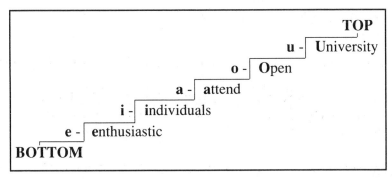

(Enthusiastic individuals attend Open University)

1)   Where more than one vowel occurs in a word, the vowel which is **highest** in the phonetic scale is retained; any remaining **lower** vowels are **deleted**.

Example: REDUNDANT = **RDUNDNT**
        The vowel **'u'** is higher in the phonetic scale than the vowels **'e'** and **'a'**; the vowel **'u'** is retained and the vowels **'e'** and **'a'** are deleted.

Exercise 1.
        Abbreviate the following words by retaining the **highest vowel only**, according to the **phonetic scale:**

        dIffer*, fIlter, shIver, bAttle*, lAment, dismAntle, bOther, devOte, diplOmat, mOney, renOvate, bUngalow, pUzzle*, rUstic, mUltiple
        No double letters

2)   Where the **commencing** vowel is **higher** in the phonetic scale than the
      rest of the vowels occurring in the word, the **commencing vowel only** is
      retained; all the remaining lower vowels are deleted.

Example: AMENITY = **AMNTY**
      The commencing vowel **'a'** is higher in the phonetic scale than the vowels
      'e' and **'i'**; the lower vowels **'e'** and **'i'** are deleted.

Exercise 2.
      Abbreviate the following words retaining the **commencing vowel only**:

      Item, Idle, Ability, Affinity*, Attend*, Annex*, Offer, Obligate, Objective,
      Obstacle, Open, Order, Optimist, Utility, Under, Understand, Utter*.
      No double letters

3)   Where the **commencing vowel** is **lower** in the phonetic scale than the
      other vowels occurring in the word, both the **commencing** vowel and the
      highest vowel are retained; any remaining vowels are deleted.

Example: ELECTRONIC = **ELCTRONC**
      The **commencing vowel 'e'** is lower in the phonetic scale than the **highest
      vowel 'o'**; the commencing vowel **'e'** and the vowel **'o'** are both retained.

Exercise 3.
      Abbreviate the following words retaining both the **commencing vowel**
      and the **highest vowel** in each word; any remaining vowels are deleted:-

      EvAde, ErOde, ErrAtic*, EmOtive, EvOlve, AdvOcate, AbOrtive,
      ImmObile*, IrrevOcable*, IgnOre, AmOrtize.
      No double letters

REPEATED VOWELS

1)   Where a vowel other than '**o**' or '**u**' is **repeated** in a word it is **deleted throughout**.

Examples:

Word	Repeated Vowel	Agiliwriting
dependent	e	**dpndnt**
ministry	i	**mnstry**
hazard	a	**hzrd**

Exercise 1.
The vowel '**e**'.
Delete the vowel '**e**' throughout in the following words:

better, between, clever, herself, letter, level, neglected, never, nevertheless, present, pretend, prevent, relented, render, renew, reveller, telex, western.
*No double letters

Exercise 2.
The vowel '**i**'.
Delete the vowel '**i**' throughout in the following words:

civic*, civil*, civility*, critic, clinic, dignity, diminish, finish, minister, signify, timid, timidity, victim.
The soft sound of 'c**' = '**s**'.

Exercise 3.
The vowel '**a**'.
Delete the vowel '**a**' throughout in the following words:

canal, cavalry, fantasy, haphazard, hazard, madam, standard, vagrant, vandal.

2)   Where a word **commences** with a vowel other than **'o'** or **'u'** and that
        vowel is **repeated** in a word, only the **commencing vowel is retained**,
        deleting all other vowels throughout.

        Examples: event = **evnt**,   adapt = **adpt**

Exercise 4.
        Abbreviate the following words retaining the **commencing vowel only**:
        No double letters

        Effect, Eject, Elect, Erect, Event, Adapt, Attach, Attract, Award

THE VOWEL 'i'

The vowel **'i'** has two distinctly different sounds; the **short-hard** sound of **'i'**
as in the word **'bit'** and the **long-soft** sound of **'i'** as in the word **'bite'**.

i)   In words containing the **short-hard** sound of **'i'**, the **'i'** remains unchanged.
ii)   In words containing the **long-soft** sound of **'i'**, the **'i'** is replaced by **'y'**.

        Examples:-
            short-hard sound of **'i'** = **'i'**:   bit = **bit**
            long-soft sound of   **'i'** = **'y'**: bite = **byt**
        *silent vowel **'e'** is deleted.

iii) In words commencing with the vowel **'i'** - the vowel **'i'** remains unchanged.

        Examples:-
        ill = **il**
        item = **itm**
        No double letters
        *The vowel **'i'** is the highest vowel in this case.

Exercise 1.
        Abbreviate the following words retaining the **short-hard** sound of the
        vowel **'i'** as **'i'**; any other vowels are deleted:-
        No double letters

        brittle, differ, fiddle, filter, hidden, litter, riddle, shiver, tipped, winner

Exercise 2.

Abbreviate the following words replacing the **long-soft** sound of the vowel **'i'** by **'y'**; any other vowels are deleted:

bide, crime, dine, dive, diver, fire, hide, hire, line, mine, rifle, wide, widen, while*.
*Silent consonant **'h'** is deleted.

Exercise 3.

Abbreviate the following words **retaining the commencing vowel 'i' as 'i'**; any other vowels are deleted:-

Idle, Identify, Ill*, Irrespective*, Item
*No double letters

Exercise 4.

Abbreviate the following words replacing the **long-soft** sound of the vowel **'i'** by **'y'**; retain the **commencing vowel** and deleting the vowel **'e'** terminating each word:

abide, afire, ignite, unite

Where words contain the **long-soft** sound of **'i'** linked to a **silent vowel and/or silent consonants,** as in the combinations - **'eigh', 'ie', 'igh', 'ui', the combinations are represented by 'y'.**

Examples: height = hyt   slight = slyt

Exercise 5.

Abbreviate the following words by replacing the combinations - **'eigh', 'ie', 'igh', 'ui',** by **'y'**, and deleting any other vowels.

bright, fight, guide, heighten, lie, tied, replied, tight, tighten.

Exercise 6.

Retain the commencing vowel and replace the combination **'ie'** by **'y'**:

allied, applied
*No double letters

THE VOWEL 'U'

The vowel **'u'** has **two** sounds - the **short-hard** sound of the vowel **'u'** as in the word **'tub'** and the **long-soft** sound of the vowel **'u'** as in the word **'tube'**.

i)   Words containing the **short-hard** sound of the vowel **'u'** - the **'u'** remains unchanged.
ii) Words containing the **long-soft** sound of the vowel **'u'** - the **'u'** is represented by **'w'**:-

Examples:

short-hard sound:	tub	= **twb**
long-soft sound:	tube	= **twb**

iii) Words **commencing** with the vowel **'u'** - the **'u'** remains unchanged.

Examples:

under = **undr**
utility = **utlty**

*Remember that the vowel **'u'** is the highest vowel in the phonetic scale so all other vowels are deleted.

Exercise 1.

Abbreviate the following words retaining the **short-hard** sound of the vowel **'u'** as **'u'**, and deleting any other vowels.
No double letters

bUffer, bUndle, bUtter, dedUct, fUndamental, redUndant, sUmmer

Exercise 2.

Abbreviate the following words by replacing the **long-soft** sound of the vowel **'u'** by **'w'** and deleting any other vowels.
No double letters

bUgle, brUtal, commUte, compUte, compUter, refUte, stUdent, tUtor

Exercise 3.
Abbreviate the following words retaining the commencing vowel **'u'** as **'u'** and deleting any other vowels.
No double letters

Under, Understand, Upward, Upper*, Unless*, Ultimate, Unify, Utensil, Unit, Unity, Urban, Urbanity, Utility.

Exercise 4.
Abbreviate the following words by replacing the **long-soft** sound of **'u'** by **'w'**; retaining the **commencing vowel** and deleting any other vowels.
No double letters

AcUte, AstUte, AttUned*, ImmUne*, ImmUtable*, ObscUre, ObscUrity, ObtrUde

DIPTHONGS 1.

These are vowels which are **linked together** to produce **two sounds** as in the words 'create' and 'virtual'.

Where the **first vowel** in a **dipthong** is either **'e'** or **'i'** - as in, **'ea'**, **'ie'**, **'ia'**, **'iou'**, **'iu'**, etc., the **dipthong vowels** are replaced by **'y'**; any remaining vowels are deleted, except for the **commencing vowel** and **'o'** or **'u'**.

Examples:

Word	Dipthong	Agiliwriting
create	ea = y	cryt
jovial	ia = y	jovyl
Orient	ie = y	Orynt

Exercise 1.

Replace the **dipthong vowels** by '**y**' and delete the remaining vowels except for '**o**' or '**u**'.
*No double letters

deviate, diary, diet, million, material, mediate, permeate, proverbial, rebellion, reliable, theatre, secretarial, violent.

Exercise 2.

*Where '**s**' occurs at the end of a word it is replaced by '**z**':

Example: furious = furyz

i)   Replace the **dipthong** vowels with '**y**'.
ii) Replace '**s**' **ending** each word with '**z**'
iii) Delete any remaining vowels.

previous, rebellious,* serious
*No double letters

Exercise 3.

Replace the **dipthong** vowels by '**y**' and retain the commencing vowel; any other vowels are deleted.
*No double letters

abbreviate, alleviate, immediate, onion, oriental, ulterior, union, oblivion, oblivious*.
*'s' at the end of a word changes to '**z**'.

DIPTHONGS 2

Where the **first vowel** in a **dipthong** is '**o**' or '**u**', as in - '**oe**', '**ue**', '**ui**', '**ua**', '**uou**', etc., the **dipthong vowels** are replaced by '**w**'; any remaining vowels are **deleted** except for the **commencing vowel** and '**o**' or '**u**'.

Examples:

Word	*Dipthong*	*Agiliwriting*
fluctuate	ua = w	**fluctwt**
poem	oe = w	**pwm**
affluent	ue = w	**aflwnt***

*No double letters

Exercise 1.

Replace the **dipthong** vowels by **'w'** and **delete** any remaining vowels except for **'o'** or **'u'**.

cr<u>ue</u>lty, fl<u>ui</u>d, fl<u>ue</u>nt, fl<u>uctua</u>ted   perpet<u>ua</u>l, p<u>oe</u>try, r<u>ui</u>n, virt<u>ua</u>l, virt<u>uou</u>s*

*'s' at the end of a word changes to **'z'**

Exercise 2.

Replace the **dipthong** vowels by **'w'**.
   Prefix: 'con = cn'

contin<u>ue</u>d, contin<u>ua</u>l, contin<u>uou</u>s*, conspic<u>uou</u>s*.
* 's' at the end of a word changes to **'z'**.

Exercise 3.

Replace the **dipthong** vowels by **'w'**, retaining the commencing vowel; any other vowels are deleted.
No double letters

aff<u>lue</u>nt, <u>a</u>nn<u>ua</u>l, a<u>c</u>cr<u>ua</u>l, act<u>ua</u>l, <u>e</u>val<u>ua</u>te, <u>e</u>vac<u>ua</u>te, <u>o</u>bit<u>ua</u>ry

LINKED VOWELS

These are vowels which are **linked together** to produce only **one sound**, for example - **'oa'** as in the word **'broad'** and **'ou'** as in the word **'found'**.

1. **Linked vowels** such as - **'au'**, **'oa'**, **'oi'**, **'oo'**, **'ou'**, etc., are represented by **'w'**.

Examples:

Word	Linked Vowels	Agiliwriting
broad	oa = w	brwd
found	ou = w	fwnd
laundry	au = w	lwndry

Exercise 1.

Replace the **'linked vowels'** by **'w'**, **deleting** any other vowels:-

boiler, book, boost, bound, boundary, cool, couch, count, counter, fault, flounder, fraud, fruit, launder, look, loud, loan, mount, point, pound, proud, round, stood, toast, took, vault.

Exercise 2.

Replace the **'linked vowels'** by **'w'**, retaining the **commencing** vowel; delete any remaining vowels.

about, abroad, abound, account, aloud, amount, around, astound, understood.

2.   The combinations **'augh'** and **'ough'** as in **'caught'** and **'bought'** are represented by **'aw'**.

Examples:

Word	*Combinations*	*Agiliwriting*
bought	**ough = aw**	**bawt**
caught	**augh = aw**	**cawt**

Exercise 3.

Replace the combinations - **'augh' and 'ough'** by **'aw'**; **delete** any other vowels:-

brought, fought, daughter, distraught, haughty, naughty, slaughter, sought, taught

SHORTS

These are frequently used words which are easily recognisable in their abbreviated form and can be as short as one character. Words in this category have to be **memorised** as they do not conform to the rules applicable to the **deletion of the vowels** as apart from the commencing vowel, they contain **consonants*** only.

*Exceptions:
our = ur, you = u

Exercise 1.
> **Delete all the vowels** in the following **'Shorts'**:-
> **No double letters*
>
> **can, come, correspond, customer, daily, day, did, done, from, kind, get, gone, happy, hope, her, him, himself, his, in, is, none, possible, some, soon, very, way.**

Exercise 2.
> **Delete** all the vowels in the following **'Shorts'**.
> Add the **suffix - 'ing = g'**:
>
> **bank/ing, cash/ing, credit/ing, find/ing, market/ing, mov/ing, part/ing, remov/ing, say/ing, tak/ing, wait/ing.**

Exercise 3.
> The following sentences are made up of words which come under the category of **'Shorts'**.
> Re-write the words in these sentences **deleting all vowels**:
> ***No double letters:**

a)   **We have banked the credits sent today in the post.**
b)   **They say they will deliver the weekly news magazine to me.**
c)   **The directors will be making many journeys to London this year.**
d)   **The two guests will leave the double room in the hotel before next Monday.**
e)   **We are happy to write that we have now sent the cheque to the customer in Winchester.**
f)   **We think that the weekly rental figure is soon to be doubled.**

STRINGS

Exercise 1.
   Read and copy the following 'Strings':

1)   we are in receipt of your letter of/**wrnrvylv**
2)   above mentioned order number/**abvmnono**
3)   we are doing all we can/**wrdglwcn**
4)   next few days/**nxfwdys**
5)   as soon as/**asns**
6)   we are able/**wrabl**
7)   delivery date/**dlvdt**
8)   we will let you know/**wwltuno**
9)   in the meantime/**nthmntm**
10) sincere apologies/**snzrapls**
11) any inconvenience/**nyncnv**
12) in this matter/**nthsmtr**

Exercise 2.
   Read and copy:-

   Agiliwriting - BASIC SHORTHAND

Dsrs,
Y Ordr No. 2065
W r n rzt v y ltr v 12 Sptmbr cnsrng th abv mnznd ordr no. W r dwng
al w cn t xpdyt y ordr f dlvry wthn th nxt fw dys nd as sn as w r abl
t gv u a fhm dlvry dt w wl lt u kno.
N th mntm, pls acpt ur snzr apljys f ny ncnvnynz czd t u n ths matr.
Yf,
Srvz Mnjr
Dzpch Dpt

Exercise 3.
Read and copy - Agiliwriting - basic shorthand, including 'STRINGS':

Dsrs,
Yono 2065
Wrnrvylv 12 Sptmbr cnsrng th abvmnono. Wrdglwcn t xpdyt y ordr
f dlvry wthn th nxfwdys nd asns wrabl t gvu a fhm dlvdt wwltuno.
Nthmntm, pls acpt ur snzrapls f nyncnv czd tu nthsmtr.
Yf,
Srvz Mnjr
Dzpch Dpt

Dear Sirs,
Your Order No.2065
We are in receipt of your letter of 12th September, concerning the *above mentioned order number. We are doing all we can* to expedite your order for delivery *within the next few days* and *as soon as we are able* to *give you* a firm *delivery date, we will let you know.*
In the meantime, please accept our *sincere apologies* for *any inconvenience* caused to you *in this matter.*
Yours faithfully,
Service Manager
Despatch Department

(*'**Strings**' are *italicised*)

NB. Answers to these exercises can be found at the end of this book.

The automatic computer transcription of **AgiliWriting** shorthand into full English Language

*Refer to end of book.

CHAPTER 3

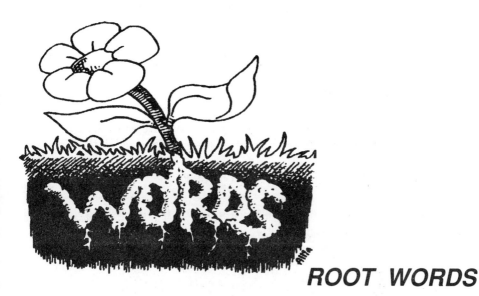

ROOT WORDS

1.   A **ROOT WORD** is a word to which is added a **prefix** and /or **suffix**, or, a **termination,** to extend its meaning.
2.   A **root word** can hold **one vowel,** or **consonants only.**
3.   Where a **root word** holding a vowel is extended - **only the vowel in the root word is retained.**

Example 1.

    ROOT WORD: **FUND = FUND**

    In the word - **REFUNDING**

        ' re' = PREFIX   **'r' = Abbreviation of PREFIX**
        'ing' = SUFFIX   **'g' = Abbreviation of SUFFIX**

    REFUNDING = re/fund/ing = RFUNDG

    In the word - **FUNDAMENTAL**

    i)   The **termination - 'mental = mntl'**
    ii) **The vowel 'u'** is the **highest vowel** according to the **phonetic scale** applicable to the **deletion of the vowels.**

    FUNDAMENTAL = fund/a/mental = **FUNDMNTL**

Example 2.

> ROOT WORD: SENT = SNT   (en = n)

In the word - **CONSENTING**

> 'con' = **PREFIX**   'cn' = abbreviation of **PREFIX**
> 'ing' = **SUFFIX**   'g' = abbreviation of **SUFFIX**

CONSENTING = con/sent/ing = CNSNTG

*Where the root word holds consonants only, all vowels, apart from the commencing vowel, are deleted.

> serve = **srv**   ob/**serve** = **obsrv**
> con/**serv**/atory = **cnsrvtry**   ('con = cn')
> con/**serv**/ing = **cnsrvg**   ('ing = g')

EXERCISE 1.

Extend the **abbreviated ROOT WORD** by applying the **abbreviated PREFIXES** and **SUFFIXES.**

*No double letters

ROOT WORD: ATTACH = ATCH*

> **Suffixes: 'ing = g',   'ment = mnt'**

ATTACH/ing, ATTACH/ment

*(See **Chapter 6** on **'Repeated Vowels'**).

EXERCISE 2

Extend the abbreviated **ROOT WORD** by applying the abbreviated **PREFIXES and SUFFIXES.**

ROOT WORD: **ROLE = ROL**

     Prefix: 'en = n'
     Suffixes: 'ing = g', 'ment = m'

en/ROL, en/ROL/ing, en/ROL/ment

EXERCISE 3.

Extend the abbreviated **ROOT WORD by applying the abbreviated PREFIXES** and **SUFFIXES.**

ROOT WORD: **PLACE = PLAZ**
                        ('c' = 'z')

   Prefixes: 'dis = ds',   're = r'
   Suffix: 'ing = g' , 'ment = m'

     dis/PLACE,   **dis/PLAC/ing,**   **dis/PLACE/ment**
     re/PLACE,   **re/PLAC/ing,**   **re/PLACE/ment**

EXERCISE 4.

Extend the abbreviated **ROOT WORD by applying the abbreviated PREFIXES** and **SUFFIXES.**

ROOT WORD: **MISSION = MZN**

     Prefixes: 'com = cm', 'per = pr', 're = r', 'sub = sb', 'inter = ntr'

    com/MISSION*,   **per/MISSION**
    re/MISSION,   **sub/MISSION**
                  inter/MISSION

*No double letters - retain one **'m'** only

Retain the **prefix vowel only:-**

                       e/MISSION

EXERCISE 5.

Extend the abbreviated **ROOT WORD** by applying the abbreviated **PRE-FIXES and SUFFIXES.**

     ROOT WORD: **TEND = TND (en=n)**

       Prefixes: 'con' = cn', 'dis = ds', 'ex = x', 'in = n'
       Suffixes: 'ing = g', 'sion/tion' = zn'

con/TEND,	**con/TEND/ing,**	**con/TEN/tion**
dis/TEND,	**dis/TEND/ing,**	**dis/TEN/tion**
ex/TEND,	**ex/TEND/ing,**	**ex/TEN/sion**
in/TEND,	**in/TEND/ing,**	**in/TEN/tion**

Retain the prefix vowel only:

            at/TEND*, at/TEND/ing, at/TEN/tion

*No double letters - retain one **'t'** only.

EXERCISE 6.

Extend the **abbreviated ROOT WORD by applying the abbreviated PRE-FIXES and SUFFIXES.**

     ROOT WORD: **LODGE = LOJ**
                                 ('dg' = j')

       Prefix: 'dis = ds'
       Suffix: 'ing = g', 'ment = m'

     dis/LODGE, dis/LODG/ing, dis/LODG/ment

N.B. lodged = **lojd**, lodger = **lojr**

CHAPTER 4

PREFIXES, SUFFIXES & TERMINATIONS

Agiliwriting abbreviates **prefixes, suffixes** and **terminations**.
In ordinary longhand, suffixes and terminations which sound the same, are spelt differently but, as **Agiliwriting** is a **phonetic** shorthand, syllables or combinations of letters which **SOUND** alike are given similar abbreviations, as shown in the following examples:-

Word	Prefix	Termination	Agiliwriting
confes/sion	con = cn	sion = zn	**cnfzn**
expedi/tion	ex = x	tion = zn	**xpdzn**
in/vent/**ing**	in = n	ing = g	**nvntg**
ex/cite/**ment**	ex = x	ment = m	**xytm**
con/scious	con = cn	scious = shz	**cnshz**
in/fec/**tious**	in = n	tious = shz	**nfcshz**
so/**cial**		cial = zl	**sozl**
sub/stan/**tial**	sub = sb	tial = zl	**sbstnzl**

Read and practice the examples given in **'LISTS'** of **Prefixes, Suffixes & Terminations**

CHAPTER 5

VOWELS IN ONE-SYLLABLE WORDS

SHORT-HARD VOWELS

Where a word contains a **single short-hard vowel**, the vowel is retained.

Word	Short-Hard Vowel	Agiliwriting
red	e = e	red
rid	i = i	rid
rat	a = a	rat
rob	o = o	rob
rub	u = u	rub

LONG-SOFT VOWELS

The vowels are eliminated, retained, or replaced, as follows:-

Word	Long-Soft Vowels	Agiliwriting
be	'e' is deleted	b
been	'ee' is deleted	bn
read	'ea' is deleted	rd

Word	Long-Soft Vowels	Agiliwriting
ride	'i' = 'y'	ryd*
rate	'a' = 'h'	rht*
raid	'ai' = 'h'	rhd
role	'o' = 'o'	rol*
rule	'u' = 'w'	rwl*

*silent vowel 'e' is deleted

*Exceptions
'Shorts' - all vowels are deleted.
(Refer to the dictionary of Shorts)

1. SHORT-HARD VOWELS 'e', 'ea' = 'e'

Examples

end = **end,** ebb = **eb*****, edge* = **ej**, egg = **eg**
debt = **det***, fell* = **fel**, wet = **wet**
breath = **breth**, head = **hed**, spread = **spred,** stealth = **stelth**
*'dg' = 'j'
*Silent consonant **'b'** is deleted
*Double letters become single letters
Exceptions
'Shorts' - all vowels are deleted.
Examples:

*fetch = fch, friend = frnd, get = gt, health = hlth, help - hlp, let = lt,
sell = sl, set = zt, wealth = wlth, etc.*

2. LONG-SOFT VOWELS 'e', 'ee', 'ea', 'ie' are deleted.

Examples:

he = **h**, me = **m**
feet = **ft**, keep = **kp**, meet = **mt,**
beat = **bt**, clear = **clr**, dream = **drm,**
heal = **hl**, lead = **ld**, meal = **ml**
please = **pls**, reach = **rch**, treat = **trt**
brief = **brf, field = fld**

Where the long-soft vowels **'ea'** **commence a word** they are represented by **'e'**:-

Examples:
each = **ech,** earn = **ern,** earth = **erth,**
ease = **ez,** eat = **et**
NB. **'eye = ey'**

3. SHORT-HARD VOWEL 'i' = 'i'

Examples:
if = **if,** ill = **il,** ink = **ink,** it = **it**
bit = **bit,** grip = **grip,** lid = **lid**
mill = **mil,** sit = **sit**

Exceptions: **'Shorts'** - all vowels are deleted
Examples:
bill = bl, did = dd, fill = fl, him = hm,·his = hs, in = n, is = s, kill = kl,
milk = mlk, skill = skl, will = wl, etc.

4. LONG-SOFT VOWEL 'i' = 'y'.

Examples:
Silent vowel **'e'** terminating each word, is deleted**:-**

bride = **bryd,** dine = **dyn,** file = **fyl**
fine = **fyn,** fire = **fyr,** hide = **hyd,**
knife* = **nyf,** line = **lyn,** site = **syt,**
tide = **tyd,** wine = **wyn,** wife = **wyf**
*'kn = n'

5. THE LONG-SOFT SOUND OF THE VOWEL 'i' LINKED TO SILENT VOWELS & CONSONANTS:

Where the **'long-soft'** **sound of the vowel 'i' is linked to a silent vowel and/ or silent consonants** as in the combinations - **'ie', 'ui', 'igh', 'eigh'**, the combinations are represented by **'y'**:

Examples:
died = **dyd,** guide = **gyd*,** guile = **gyl***
fright = **fryt,** lied = **lyd,** tried = **tryd**
light = **lyt,** height = **hyt,** tight = **tyt**
*silent vowel **'e'** is deleted.

Exceptions
'Shorts' - all vowels are deleted.
Examples:
find=fnd, kind = knd, like=lk, rise = rz, side = sd, size = sz, write = wrt, etc.

6. SHORT-HARD VOWELS 'a', 'ea', = 'a'

Examples:
    add = **ad**, all = **al**, am = **am**, art = **art**, as = **as**
    ask = **ask,** far = **far**, hat = **hat**, rat = **rat**
    raw = **raw**, war = **war**, heart = **hart**

Exceptions
'Shorts' - all vowels are deleted.
Examples:
    and = nd, any = ny, are = r, bank = bnk, can = cn,
    cash = csh, had = hd, has = hz,have = hv, half = hf, halve = hlv,
    mark = mrk, part = prt, saw = zw, etc.

7. The long-soft vowels 'a', 'ai', 'ea' = 'h'.

Examples:
    fate = **fht**, late = **lht**, rate = **rht**
    bail = **bhl**, fair = **fhr**, laid = **lhd**, main = **mhn**
    raid = **rhd**, rain = **rhn**, raise* = **rhz**
    strain = **strhn**, str<u>aigh</u>t* = **strht**
    fr<u>eigh</u>t* = **frht**, great = **grht**

    ***eigh', 'aigh' = 'h'**

Exceptions:
i)   The consonant **'h'** representing the vowel **'a'** cannot
    follow **'c', 'ch', 'h', 'p', 's', 't'.**
    All the vowels are deleted in some words following these consonants: i.e.
    chair = chr, paid = pd, pay = py, pair = pr, share = shr, stair = str, etc.

ii)   The vowel **'a'** is retained as **'a'**:
    came = cam, hair = har, hate* = hat, hail* = hal,*
    scale = scal, shade = shad, etc.
    'h' cannot follow 'h'.

iii) The vowel **'a'** is retained as **'a'** in some words where this vowel follows **'linked consonants'**.
blame = blam, brave = brav, flame = flam, grade = grad, grave = grav, place* = plaz, plate = plat, praise = praz*, trace = traz*, etc.
*'c' changes to 'z'

iv) Where the vowel **'a'** is linked to the consonant **'y'** as in the word — **'day'**, this combination is represented by **'y'**, thus:
day = **dy**, lay = **ly,** may = **my,** pay = **py,** say = **sy**

v) **'Shorts'** — all vowels are deleted.
date = dt, made = md, make = mk, paid = pd, save = sv, wait = wt.

8) The SHORT-HARD VOWEL 'o' = 'o'.

Examples:
on = **on**, or = **or,** out = **ot**, ought = **owt**
bond = **bond**, cot = **cot**, drop = **drop**, fox = **fox**
slot = **slot**, solve = **solv**, top = **top**
block* = **blok**, lock* = **lok**, stock* = **stok**

*'ck = k'
*'off = ov'

Exceptions
'Shorts' - all vowels are deleted.
Examples:
come = cm, done = dn, gone = gn, not = nt, of = v, some = sm, etc.

N.B. Where the **short-hard** sound of the vowel **'o'** and the **long-soft sound** of the vowel **'o'** lie between identical consonants, **the long-soft sound of the vowel 'o' can change to 'w' to avoid identical abbreviations:-**

short-hard sound	long-soft sound
cod = **cod**	code = **cwd**
rob = **rob**	robe = **rwb**
rod = **rod**	rode = **rwd**
clock = **clok**	cloak = **clwk**
cloth = **cloth**	clothe = **clwth**

9. The LONG-SOFT VOWELS 'oo'. 'oa', 'oi', 'ou', etc.

These vowels are replaced by **'w'**. (See chapter 'Linked Vowels').

Examples:
book = **bwk**, look = **lwk,** shook - **shwk**, took = **twk**
broad = **brwd**, foil = **fwl**, load = **lwd**, loan = **lwn**
count = **cwnt**, hound = **hwnd**, pound = **pwnd**
round = **rwnd**, sound = **zwnd***

*'s' changes to **'z'** when followed by **'w'**

Exceptions:
Shorts - all vowels are deleted.

Examples:
could = cd, hope = hp, low = lw, road = rd, room = rm, row = rw,
soon = sn, should = shd, would = wd, etc.

10. ONE-SYLLABLE WORDS HOLDING LINKED VOWELS AND CONSONANTS:

In these words, **'augh'** and **'ough'** are represented by **'aw'**.

Examples:
caught = **cawt,** taught = tawt
fought = fawt, nought = **nawt,** sought = **sawt**

Exception:
draught = drwft

11. SHORT-HARD VOWEL 'u' = 'u'

Examples:
up = **up,** us = **us**, cut = **cut**, fund = **fund**, tub = **tub**

12. LONG-SOFT VOWEL 'u' = 'w'.

Examples:
cube = **cwb**, fuse* = **fwz**, rule = **rwl**, tube = **twb**, use = **uz**
*Where **'s'** ends a word it changes to **'z'**.
The consonant **'s'** is added in plurals.
'fuse<u>s</u> = **fwzs**'.

13. Where the vowel 'e' occurs before the consonants 'm', 'n', 's', 'x', the vowel 'e' is deleted.

i)   'em', 'en' 'ex' = m, n, x.

Examples:
tempt = **tmpt**, be̲nch = **bnch**, Fre̲nch = **Frnch**,
le̲nd = **lnd**, length = **lnth***, re̲nt = **rnt**, spe̲nd = **spnd**, se̲nt = **snt**, te̲nt = **tnt**,
tre̲nch = **trnch**, went = **wnt**
ne̲xt = **nxt**, te̲xt = **txt**

*Silent consonant '**g**' is deleted

ii)   The vowel '**i**' is deleted when it occurs before the consonants '**m**' and '**n**'. (**in = n**)

Examples:
skimp = **skmp**, swim = **swm**,
in = **n**, bring = **brng**, drink = **drnk,** hint = **hnt**
link = **lnk**, ring = **rng**, skin = **skn,** sing = **sng**
thing = **thng**, wing = **wng**

iii) The vowels '**e**' or '**i**' are deleted when they occur before '**s**': '**es**' = '**s**' and '**is**' = '**s**'.

Examples:
best = **bst**, desk = **dsk**, less = **ls**, rest = **rst**
press = **prs**, test = **tst**, west = **wst**
list = **lst**, risk = **rsk**, twist = **twst**

Exceptions:
'**es**' = '**z**'
'**bless = blz**', '**dress = drz**'

14. COMMON SOUNDS.

Examples:

birth	(**bir = br**) = **brth,**	burn	(**bur = br**) = **brn**
dirt	(**dir = dr**) = **drt,**	dearth	(**dear = dr**) = **drth**
her	(**her = hr**) = **hr,**	hurt	(**hur = hr**) = **hrt**
learn	(**lear = lr**) = **lrn,**	lurch	(**lur = lr**) = **lrch**
perch	(**per = pr**) = **prch,**	search	(**sear = sr**) = **srch**
were	(**wer = wr**) = **wr,**	worth	(**wor = wr**) = **wrth**

15. EXTENDING ONE-SYLLABLE WORDS.

i)   The form of the **one-syllable word**, whether it is   abbreviated or unabbreviated, becomes a **ROOT WORD** and it does not **change** with the application of a **prefix and/or suffix, termination, or an additional syllable:**

ii)   A one-syllable word can hold **consonants only**, or **one vowel**.

iii)   Where a one-syllable word containing a vowel is extended - **only the vowel in the 'root word' is retained.**

Examples:

SHORT - HARD VOWELS

1)   <u>The vowels 'e' = 'e', 'ea = e'</u>
       Suffix: **'ing = g'**

       pledge = **plej***, pledged = **plejd**, pledging = **plejg**
       head = **hed**, header = **hedr,** heading = **hedg**
       *'**dg = j**'

2)   <u>'em = m'</u>
       tempt = **tmpt,** tempt/ed = **tmptd,** tempt/ing = **tmptg**

3)   <u>'en = n'</u>
       rent = **rnt,** rent/ed = **rntd,** rent/ing = **rntg**
       length = **lnth*,** lengthen = **lnthn,**
       lengthening = **lnthng**
       *Silent 'g' is deleted.**

4)   <u>'es = s'</u>
       test = **tst,** test/ed = **tstd,** test/ing = **tstg**

5)   <u>The vowel 'i' = 'i'</u>
       bid = **bid**, bidd/er* = **bidr**, bidd/ing = **bidg**
       bridge* = **brij**, bridged = **brijd**, bridging = **brijg**
       *'**dg' = 'j'**

6)   <u>'is = s'</u>
list = **lst**, list/ed = **lstd**, list/ing = **lstg**

7)   <u>'in = n'</u>
drink = **drnk**, drink/er = **drnkr**, drinking = **drnkg**

8)   <u>The vowel 'a' = 'a'</u>

Prefix   'com = cm'
Suffix: 'ing = g'

bat = **bat**, batt/ed = **batd**, batt/ing = **batg**
com/bat = **cmbat**, com/batt/ed = **cmbatd**
com/batt/ing = **cmbatg**

9)   <u>The vowel 'o' = 'o'</u>

Prefix: 'com = cm'
Suffix: 'ing = g'

block* = **blok**, block/ed - **blokd,** block/ing = **blokg**
*'ck = k'
pot = **pot**, pott/ed* = **potd**, pott/er = **potr**,
potting = **potg**, com/pot = **cmpot**

10)   <u>The vowel 'u' = 'u'</u>

cut = **cut**, cutt/er* = **cutr**, cutt/ing = **cutg**
rush = **rush**, rush/ed = **rushd**, rush/ing = **rushg**

*Remember - double letters become single letters
*The vowel **'u'** is the **highest vowel** in the phonetic scale.

LONG-SOFT VOWELS

1) <u>The vowels 'ea', 'ee' - are deleted:-</u>

   Suffixes 'ing = g', 'ment = m'

treat = **trt**, treat/ed = **trtd**, treat/ing = **trtg**, treat/ment = **trtm**

greet = **grt**, greet/ed = grtd, greet/ing = grtg

2) <u>The vowel 'i' = 'y'</u> - the lower vowel **'e'** is deleted:-

ride = **ryd***, rider = **rydr**, riding = **rydg**

<u>The combinations - 'ui', 'eigh','igh' = 'y':-</u>

fright = **fryt**, fright/en = **frytn**, frighten/ing = **frytng**
guide = **gyd,** guided = **gydd**, guiding = **gydg**
height = **hyt,** heighten = **hytn**, heightening = **hytng**

3) <u>The vowels 'a', 'ai' = 'h':-</u>

bake = **bhk**, bak/er = **bhkr**, bak/ing = **bhkg**
main = mhn, remain = **rmhn**, remain/ing = **rmhng**, remain/der = **rmhndr**
train = **trhn,** trainer = **trhnr**, training = **trhng**

<u>The vowel 'a' = 'a'</u>

Suffixes: - 'ing = g', 'ment = m'

state = **stat**,* stat/ing = **statg**, statement = **statm**

*The consonant **'h'** cannot follow **'t'**

4) <u>The vowels 'oo', 'oa', 'ou' = 'w'</u>

(See Chapter 7 on 'Linked Vowels')

book = **bwk**, book/ed = **bwkd**, book/ing = **bwkg**

broad = **brwd,** broad/er = **brwdr**, broad/est = **brwdst**, abroad = **abrwd**

count = **cwnt**, count/ed = **cwntd**, count/er = **cwntr**
ac/count = **acwnt,** ac/count/ed = **acwntd**
ac/count/ant = **acwntnt,** ac/count/ing = **acwntg**

round = **rwnd**, sur/round = **srwnd***, sur/round/ing = **srwndg,**
a/round = **arwnd**
*sur = **sr**

5) <u>The vowel 'u' = 'w'</u>

cube = **cwb**, cub/ic = **cwbc**, cub/icle = **cwbcl**
rule = **rwl**, rul/ed = **rwld,** rul/er = **rwlr**, rul/ing = **rwlg**

*No double letters
*The vowel **'u'** is the highest vowel in the phonetic scale.

CHAPTER 6

VOWELS IN WORDS
OF MORE THAN ONE SYLLABLE

Phonetic scale applicable to the **DELETION OF THE VOWELS.**

A **mnemonic** is given to help remember the vowel order.

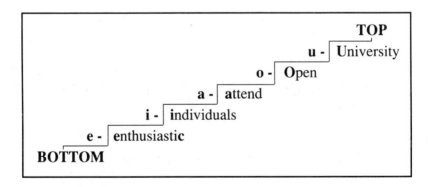

(enthusiastic individuals attend Open University)

This is demonstrated in the following examples.

Example 1.
Where more than one vowel occurs in a word, the vowel which is **highest in the scale is retained;** any other vowels are deleted:-

Word	Syllables	Highest Vowel	Agiliwriting
renovate	ren/o/vate	o	rnovt

Example 2.
Where a word **commences** with a vowel higher in the scale than the other vowel(s) occurring in the word, the **commencing vowel is retained**; any other vowels are deleted:-

Word	Syllables	Highest Vowel	Agiliwriting
amenity	a/men/i/ty	a	amnty

Example 3.
Where a word **commences** with a vowel **lower** in the scale than the highest vowel occurring in the word, **the commencing vowel and the highest vowel are retained;** any other vowels are deleted:-

Word	Syllables	Highest Vowel	Agiliwriting
abundant	a/bun/dant	u	abundnt

NB.   Additional rule:
Applicable to words of **two syllables or more,** containing **only** the short-hard vowels 'e' and 'i'; except for the **commencing** vowel, **all the vowels 'e' and 'i' are deleted.**

Examples:-

Word	Syllables	Vowels	Agiliwriting
benefit	be/ne/fit	e/e/i	bnft
deficit	de/fi/cit	e/i/i	dfzt*
electric	e/lec/tric	e/e/i	elctrc
evidence	e/vi/dence	e/i/e/e	evdnz*
flexible	flex/i/ble	e/i/e	flxbl
register	re/gi/ster	e/i/e	rjstr*
testify	tes/ti/fy	e/i	tstfy

*'c' = 'z'
*Soft 'g' = 'j'

For the following exercises, remember that there are no **double letters** used in **Agiliwriting.**

EXERCISE 1.

Retain the commencing vowel **'a'** and the highest remaining vowel; any other vowels are deleted.

admOnish, admOnish/ment (ment = **m**), abOlish
abOlish/ing (ing = **g**), abhOrent, abOrtive, allOcate,
allOca/tion (tion = **zn**), arrOgant, assUnder

EXERCISE 2.

Retain the commencing **'a'** vowel only:-

Affix, Affix/ing (ing = **g**), Amicable, Amend,
Amend/ment (ment = **m**), Animal, Anniversary, Assertive,
Asser/tion (tion = **zn**)

EXERCISE 3.

Retain the highest vowel only:-

bOttle, bUffer, bUndle, bUrrow, bUngalow, bUtter, brUtal (u = **w**)

EXERCISE 4.

Retain the highest vowel only:-

The long sound of **'u = w'**
***No double letters**
commUte, commUter,compUter,compUt/ing (ing = **g**), cUbic,
cUbicle
'u = u'
cUddle, cUtter

EXERCISE 5.

Retain the highest vowel only:-

destrUctive (**'u = u'**), destrUction (u = u,.ction = **cn**),
diffU<u>s</u>e (u = **w,** s = **z**), diffU/sion (**'u'** = **'w'**, sion = **zn**),
disrUptive (**'u = u'**), disrUpt/ing (ing = **g**)

EXERCISE 6.

Retain the commencing vowel **'e'** and the highest vowel:-

effU<u>s</u>ive (s = **z,** u = **w**), egOtistical, emOtive,
emO/tion (tion = **zn**), emO/tional (tional = **znl**)
emUl/sion   (**'u = u'**, sion = **zn**), episcOpal, errAtic,
errOtic, errO/sion (sion = **zn**), erUpt/ing (ing = **g**),
erU/ption (**'u = u'**,tion = **pn**), eq<u>u</u>Ate (qu = **q**), eq<u>u</u>ivOcal (qu = **q**), evOlve/
ment (ment = **m**)

EXERCISE 7.

Retain the highest vowel only:-

flAnnel, frUgal (u = **w**), fUrrow (**'u = u'**), flUttered,
flUtte/ring (ring = **rng**), frAgile (soft 'g' = 'j'), fUmble,
fUn/ction (ction = **cn**), fUndamental, fUgitive (**'u = w'. soft 'g' = 'j'**).

EXERCISE 8.

Retain the highest vowel only:-

gOlden,glUtton (**'u = u'**), gObble,gObbl/ing (ing = **g**),gUnner (**'u = u'**),
gUnn/ing (ing = **g**), gUtter, gUtte/ring (ring = **rng**)

EXERCISE 9.

Retain the highest vowel only:-

hAmmer, hAmme/ring (ring = **rng**), hArleq<u>u</u>in (qu = **q**),
helicOpter, hUman (u = **w**), hUmanity (u = **w**), hOrrible,
hUrricane (**'u = u'**), hypOcrite (hyp = **hp**),
hypOcritical (hyp = **hp**), hypOdermic (hyp = **hp**)

EXERCISE 10.

Retain the commencing vowel **'i'** and the highest vowel.

immUtable (u = **w**), irrevOcable, irOnical

Retain the **commencing vowel only:-**

Item, Illegible (soft 'g' = **'j'**),

EXERCISE 11.
　　Prefix 'in = n'.

　　Retain the highest vowel following 'in = n':-
　　in/sUfferable ('u = u'), in/destrUctable, in/corrUptible,
　　in/hUman (u = w), in/tOlerable, in/tOxicate,
　　in/tOxicat/ing (ing = g),in/tOxica/tion (tion = zn),
　　in/terlOper, in/vOlved, in/vOlve/ment (ment = m).

EXERCISE 12.
　　Retain the highest vowel only:

　　jObber, jObb/ing (ing = g), jUmper ('u = u'), jump/ing(ing = g),
　　jAgged, jUbilant (u = w), jUngle

EXERCISE 13.
　　Retain the highest vowel only:-

　　lAnded, lAnd/ing (ing = g), lApped, lOgic (soft 'g' = 'j'), lOgical (soft 'g'
　　= 'j'), lOgistic (soft 'g' = 'j'),lUggage ('u = u', soft 'g' = 'j'), lOver,
　　lOv/ing (ing = g), lUbricate (u = w), lUbrica/tion (tion = zn)

EXERCISE 14.
　　Retain the highest vowel.

　　mAtter, memO, mOdern, mOder/nise (nise = nz),
　　mOrtgage (soft 'g' = 'j'), mOther, mOttled, mUddle ('u = u'),
　　mUsic (u = w)

EXERCISE 15.
　　Retain the highest vowel only:-

　　nIpple, nOble, nObility, nUmerable (u = 'w'), nOtion (tion = zn)

EXERCISE 16.
　　Retain the commencing vowel 'o' only:-

　　Obey, Obligate, Obliga/tion(tion = zn), Observe, Observ/ing(ing = g),
　　Omitted, Order, Orde/ring (ring = rng), Ordinarily, Open, Open/ing
　　(ing = g), Other, Otherwise ('s' = 'z'), Over, Overdraft, Owner,
　　Ownership

EXERCISE 17.

Retain the highest vowel only:-

pOlitical, pOtentate, prOsper, prOsperity, pOttery, prOdigal, prOffer,prOfit,prOfitable,prOgramme, prOgramm/ing (ing = **g**),prOgrammer,prOvencal

EXERCISE 18.

Retain the highest vowel:-

remOte, revOke, revOk/ing (ing = **g**), revOlve, revOlver, rUbber (**'u = u'**), rUbb/ing (ing = **g**), rUbbish,redUndant, refUnd, refUndable, refUnd/ing (ing = **g**), rUle ('u' = **'w'**), rUler ('u' = **'w'**), rUl/ing ('u' = **'w'**, 'ing = **g**)

EXERCISE 19.

Retain the highest vowel:-

shOpper, shOpp/ing (ing -= **g**), shUffle (**'u = u'**), sOcket (**'ck = k'**),   sOlitary, sOlitaire, stAble, stAbility, stAmped, stOcked ('ck' = **'k'**), stOck/ing (ck = **k,** ing = **g**), sUdden (**'u = u'**), sUffer, sUmmer

EXERCISE 20.

Retain the highest vowel only:-

tOlerable, tOlerant, tOpped, tOpp/ing (ing = **g**), tOrrent, tOrren/tial (tial = **zl**), tOnality,trOpic, trOpical

EXERCISE 21.

Retain the commencing vowel **'u'** = **'u'** only.

Under, Understand, Understand/ing (ing = **g**), Urgent (soft 'g' = **'j'**), Undeserved, Unlimited, Universe ('s' = **'z'**), University ('s' = **'z'**), Unworkable, Urban, Utility

EXERCISE 22.

Retain the highest vowel only:-

vOcal, vOltage (soft 'g' = **'j'**), vUlgar (**'u - u'**), vUlgarity, vUlnerable

EXERCISE 23 - Additional Rule applicable to deletion of the vowels in words of two or more syllables.

Delete all the **short-hard vowels 'e'** and **'i'** except for the **commencing vowel:-**

benefit, certify (soft 'c' = 's'), definite, electric, feminism, gifted, hinder, immense ('s' = 'z'), linger, metric, perspective, resident, silver, ticket ('ck = k'), vestige, witness ('ss' = 'z')

CHAPTER 7

REPEATED VOWELS

Where a vowel, other than '**o**' or '**u**' is **repeated** in a word it is **deleted throughout**.

Examples:

Word	Repeated Vowel	Agiliwriting
between	*e*	**bt**w**n**
finish	i	**fnsh**
stand**ard**	a	**stndrd**

Where a word **commences** with a vowel and the vowel is **repeated** in a word; only the **commencing** vowel is retained:

Examples:

Word	Repeated Vowels	Agiliwriting
eleven	e	**elvn**
immit*	i	**imt**
adamant	a	**admnt**
*No double letters		

EXERCISE 1.

Delete the vowel 'e' throughout:
*Remember, in the following exercises, no double letters should appear.

> **beget, better, betterment, defer, deference*, deject, delete, depend, depended, dependent, deplet, depleted, fever, helper, herself, jewel, jeweller, jewellery, keeper, letter, level, levelled, neglect, never, nevertheless, perfect, prefer, preference*, present, presented, pretend, pretended, pretence,* rebel, refer, referring, reference*, regret, regretted, relent, relentless, remember, renew, renewed, repel, repellent, repent, repented, respect, respected, resplendent, revel, reveller, revenge*, reverence*, revert, reverted, secret, secretly, select, selfless, sentence*, September, seven, seventy, telex, tender, weekend, western.**

* 'c' changes to 'z'
* The soft sound of **'g' = 'j'**

N.B.   decent = **dznt**, descend = **dsnd**, descent = **dsnt**
        recede = **rzd**, recent = **rsnt**, resent = **rznt**
        redress = **rdrz***

EXERCISE 2.

Retain the **commencing vowel only**:
*No double letters

Example: erect = **erct**

> **ebbed, effect, eleven, emerge*, emergency*, elect, endless, even, event, every.**

*The soft sound of **'g' = 'j'**
*'c' changes to **'z'**.

EXERCISE 3.

'ex = x'

Delete the vowel **'e' throughout, commencing** each word with **'ex = x'**.

Example: expend = **xpnd**

expect, expected, expert, extend, extended, extent, exempt, expence*, expences*, extreme, extremely.

*'c' changes to 'z'.
*'s' is added in **plurals**:-

essence = **esnz**, essences = **esnzs**

N.B.   excel = **xl**, excellent = **xlnt**

EXERCISE 4.

Copy the following examples:-

'qu = q'

equerry = **eqry**
bequest = **bqst**, bequested = **bqstd**
request = **rqst**, requested = **rqstd**

EXERCISE 5.

Copy the following examples:-

The linked vowels - **'ei', 'ie', 'ea',** found in the second syllable sound like **'e'**.
All the vowels are deleted.

believe = **blv**, belief = **blf**, bereave = **brv**
deceive = **dzv**, deceit = **dzt**, defeat = **dft**
perceive* = **przv**, perceived* = **przvd**
receive* = **rzv**, receipt* = **rzt**
repeat = **rpt**, repeated = **rptd**
relieve = **rlv**, relieved = **rlvd**
relief = **rlf**, release = **rlz**
reprieve = **rprv**
*'c' = 'z'

The addition of PREFIXES and/or SUFFIXES to words holding repeated vowels:

EXERCISE 6.
Delete the vowel 'e' and replace the suffix 'ing' with 'g'.
*No double letters.

> **delet/ing, depend/ing, levell/ing, neglect/ing, present/ing, pretend/ ing, relent/ing, represent/ing, respect/ing, revert/ing, preserv/ing, telex/ing.**

EXERCISE 7.
Retain the **commencing vowel only**:
*No double letters

> **ebb/ing, effect/ing, elect/ing, erect/ing**

EXERCISE 8.
Commence each word with 'ex = x', deleting the vowel 'e' and replace the **suffix** 'ing' with 'g'.

> <u>ex</u>pect/ing, <u>ex</u>pend/ing, <u>ex</u>empt/ing, <u>ex</u>tend/ing

EXERCISE 9.
Delete the vowel 'e' and replace the **suffix 'tion'** by 'zn'.

> dele/**tion**, deten/**tion**, reple/**tion**, reten/**tion**

EXERCISE 10.
Delete all the vowels 'e' and replace the suffix 'ring' by 'rng'.
*No double letters

> bette/**ring**, defer/**ring**, lette/**ring**, prefe/**ring**, refer/**ring**, rende/**ring**, tende/ **ring**.

EXERCISE 11.
Copy the following examples replacing the termination **'wing'** with **'wng'**:-

renew = **rnw,** renewing = **rnwng**
review = **rvw,** reviewing = **rvwng**
preview = **pryvw,** previewing = **pryvwng**

EXERCISE 12.
Delete the vowel 'e' throughout, following the format of the first worked example:

Suffix - 'ing = g'
Suffix - 'tion' following 'c' = 'cn'

deject = **djct,** deject/ing = **djctg,** deje/ction = **djcn**

neglect, neglect/**ing**, negle/**ction**
perfect, perfect/**ing**, perfe/**ction**
reject, reject/**ing**, reje/**ction**
select, select/**ing**, sele/**ction**

Retain the commencing vowel only:

elect, elect/**ing**, ele/**ction**
erect, erect/**ing**, ere/**ction**

EXERCISE 13.
Delete the vowel **'e'** **throughout**, following the format of the first worked example:-

Suffix - 'tion' following 'p' = 'pn'

Examples:
dece/**ption** = **dzpn** ('c' = 'z')
rece/**ption**, perce/**ption**

N.B. conce/ption = **cnzpn** (con = cn)
ince/ption = **nzpn** (in = n)

The Vowel 'i'.

EXERCISE 1.
Delete the vowel **'i'** throughout:

Example:- **clinic = clnc**

civic*, civil*, civility*, clinic, critic, diminish, distinct, digit*, finish, gimmick*, limit, mimic, rigid*, rigidity*, skirmish, spirit, timid, timidity, signify, victim, villify,* within.

*Soft 'c' = 's'
*Soft 'g' = 'j'
*'ck' = 'k'
*No double letters

EXERCISE 2.
Copy the following examples:-

i)   **Silent vowel 'e'** terminating each word, is deleted:
         distinctive = **dstnctv**, divide = **dvd**, vindictive = **vndctv**

ii)   **Prefix 'in' = 'n':**
         in/distinct = **ndstnct**, in/hibit = **nhbt**

iii)   When a word ends with **'s'**, this consonant changes to **'z'**. The consonant
         's' is added to indicate **plurals:-**
         minimise = **mnmz**, minimises = **mnmzs**
         victimise = **vctmz**, victimises = **vctmzs**

iv)   **'qu' = 'q':**
         liquid = **liqd**, liquidity = **lqdty**, liquify = **lqfy**, liquidise = **lqdz**

v)   **in = n**
         in/hibit = **nhbt**, in/iquity = **nqty**
         in/quisitive = **nqztv**

vi)   When **'i' commences** a word, **'i' is retained** as **'i'**; all other vowels are
         deleted:-
         illicit* = **ilzt**, immit = **imt**
*'c' = 'z'

The addition of PREFIXES and/or SUFFIXES to words holding repeated vowels:

EXERCISE 3.
Delete the vowel **'i'** throughout and replace the **suffix 'ing'** by **'g'**.
*No double letters

diminish/**ing**, divid/**ing**, finish/**ing**, limit/**ing**, signify/**ing**, villify/**ing**.

The Vowel 'a'

EXERCISE 1.

Delete the vowel **'a' throughout**:

Example: salary = **slry**

canal, canary, haphazard, hazard, madam, rampant, rampart, rascal, scandal, vagrant, vandal

Exceptions:
The vowel **'a'** following **'r'** is retained unless the word commences with **'a'**:
attract = **atrct**, 'Radar = **Radr**', 'Ramadan = **Ramdn**'
The vowel **'a'** ending a word is retained, as in, 'Canasta = **Cnsta**'

EXERCISE 2.
Copy the following examples:-

i)   The vowel **'a'** is deleted throughout as well as the silent vowel **'e'** terminating each word.
ii)   The soft sound of **'g'** = **'j'**.
iii)   **'ck'** = **'k'**
       *No double letters

cabbage = **cbj**, damage = **dmj**, manage = **mnj**, passage = **psj**, salvage = **slvj**, savage = **svj**.
package = **pkj**

EXERCISE 3.
Retain the **commencing vowel only**:
*No double letters.

> adamant, adapt, aggravate, amalgamate, amaze, apathy, attach, attract, aware, award

The addition of PREFIXES and/or SUFFIXES to words holding repeated vowels:-

EXERCISE 4.
i) Delete all vowels.
ii) Add the Suffixes - 'ing = g', 'ment = m':-
iii) Soft consonant **'g' = 'j'**

> manag/**ing**, manage/**ment**, salvag/**ing**

EXERCISE 5.
Retain the **commencing vowel** only and replace the suffix **'ing'** by **'g'**.

> adapt/**ing**, aggravat/**ing**, amalgamat/**ing**, attach/**ing**, attract/**ing**, award/**ing**

*No double letters

THE VOWEL 'o'

Where the vowel **'o'** is repeated in a word, the vowel **'o'** in the **first syllable of the word is retained** unless the word contains - **'com = cm'** or **'con = cn'**.
*No double letters

Examples:

1)	*Word*	*Syllables*	**Agiliwriting**
	commodity	com/mo/dity	**cmodty**
	economy	e/con/omy	**ecnomy**
	condone	con/done	**cndon**
2)	cordon	cor/don	**cordn**
	cotton	cot/ton	**cotn**
	donor	do/nor	**donr**
	motor	mo/tor	**motr**
	sponsor	spon/sor	**sponsr**

2)	*Word*	*Syllables*	**Agiliwriting**
	provoke	pro/voke	**provk**
	propo<u>s</u>e*	pro/pose	**propz**

*'pro - pro'
's' = 'z'

3)	monopoly	mo/no/poly	**mnoply**
	monotony	mo/no/tony	**mnotny**

*'mono = mno'

4)	astronomy	as/tro/nomy	**astronmy**
	astronomical	as/tro/no/mical	**astronmcl**
	gastronomy	ga/stro/nomy	**gstronmy**

5)	technology	tech/no/logy	**tcnljy**
	technological	tech/no/logical	**tcnljcl**

*'ology' = 'ljy', 'ological = 'ljcl'

N.B. 'chronology = **cronljy**, 'chronicle = **croncl**'
*soft 'g' = 'j'.

Termination **'logue = log'** as in 'prologue = **prolog**', 'monologue = **mnolog**'

Word	Syllables	Agiliwriting
biology	bi/ology	**byljy**
biological	bi/o/logical	**byljcl**

Dipthong 'bio = by'

psychology	psych/ology	**sycljy**
psychological	psych/o/logical	**sycljcl**

'psy = sy' 'ch = c'

Terminations 'low = lw', 'row = rw'
*No double letters

follow	fo/low	**folw**
shallow	shal/low	**shalw**
borrow	bor/row	**borw**
sorrow	sor/row	**sorw**

THE VOWEL 'u'

Where the vowel **'u'** is repeated in a word, the vowel **'u' in the first syllable of the word is retained.**

Examples:

Word	Syllables	Agiliwriting
culture	cul/ture	**cultr**
future	fu/ture	**futr**
juncture	junc/ture	**junctr**
luxury	lux/ury	**luxry**
puncture	punc/ture	**punctr**
structure	struc/ture	**structr**
succum<u>b</u>*	suc/cumb	**sucm**

*Silent consonant 'b' is deleted.

CHAPTER 8

LINKED VOWELS

These are vowels which are **linked together** to produce only **one sound**, for example - **'ou'** as in the word **'mount'**, and **'oa'** as in the word **'broad'**.

1. The **'Linked Vowels'** - *'au', 'oa', 'oi', 'oo', 'ou', 'ui'*, are represented by **'w'**; any other vowels are deleted, with the exception of the **commencing** vowel:-

*Remember - **no double letters**

Examples:
'au': appl<u>au</u>d = **aplwd**, appl<u>au</u>se* = **aplwz**, f<u>au</u>lt = **fwlt**
'oa': l<u>oa</u>n = **lwn**, abr<u>oa</u>d = **abrwd**, br<u>oa</u>ch = **brwch**,
'oi': av<u>oi</u>d = **avwd**, dev<u>oi</u>d = **dvwd**, memoir = **mmwr**
'oo': b<u>oo</u>k = **bwk**,l<u>oo</u>k = **lwk**, t<u>oo</u>k = **twk**,
'ou': bl<u>ou</u>se = **blwz**, c<u>ou</u>p = **cw**, m<u>ou</u>nt = **mwnt**
      r<u>ou</u>tine = **rwtn**, tr<u>ou</u>ser = **trwsr**
'ui': fr<u>ui</u>t = **frwt**, s<u>ui</u>t* = **zwt**, s<u>ui</u>table* = **zwtbl**

*When 's' ends a word it changes to **'z'**.
*'s' changes to **'z'** when followed by **'w'**.

2.   The combinations of - **'augh'** and **'ough'** as in the words **'caught'** and **'bought'**, are represented by **'aw'**; any other vowels are deleted:

Examples:

>   br<u>ough</u>t = **brawt**, d<u>augh</u>ter = **dawtr,** fr<u>augh</u>t = **frawt**
>   h<u>augh</u>ty = **hawty,** l<u>augh</u>ter = **lawftr**, s<u>ough</u>t = **sawt**

Exceptions

i)   b<u>ough</u> = **bw**
       dr<u>ough</u>t = **drowt**, draught = **drwft**
       n<u>eigh</u>bour = **nhbr**
       <u>ough</u>t = **owt**

ii)   **Shorts** - all vowels are deleted:

Examples:
       cause = **cz**
       favour = **fvr**
       floor = **flr**
       fluorescent = **flrsnt**
       road = **rd**
       room = **rm**

iii)   The **'Linked Vowels'** are deleted in **'terminations'** as follows:

'w' cannot be repeated in a word:
       Thus, where a word contains a **dipthong/the long soft sound of 'u'/**
       'Linked Vowels', only the **first 'w' is retained**:

Example: r<u>ui</u>n<u>ou</u>s = **rwnz**   ('s' = 'z')

>   **Dipthong = 'ui'** in the first syllable - is represent by **'w'**
>   **'Linked Vowels' = 'ou'** - in the second syllable are **deleted.**

Examples:

Word	Syllables	Agiliwriting
connoisseur	con/nois/seur	cnwsr
credulous	cred/u/lous*	crdwlz
fortuitous	for/tui/tous*	fortwtz
ridiculous	ri/dic/u/lous	rdcwlz
voluminous	vol/u/mi/nous*	volwmnz

*'s' at the end of a word changes to 'z'.

iv)   Where the **'sound'** of the **'Linked Vowels'** in some terminations is very
      soft, the **'linked vowels'** are deleted:

<u>soft-sound</u>
      armour = **armr**
      endeavour = **ndvr**   (en = n)
      valour = **valr**

v)   <u>hard-sound</u>
      The **'linked vowels'** are replaced by **'w'**.

      amour = **amwr**
      valorous = **valrwz***
      ominous = **omnwz***
      *'s' = 'z'

vi)   Where a word contains the vowel **'o'** followed by the consonant **'w'**, the
      vowel **'o'** and any other vowels are deleted, as shown in the following
      examples:-

      crowd = **crwd**, flower = **flwr**, lower = **lwr**
      shower = **shwr**, power = **pwr**, tower = **twr**

      The **commencing vowel** is retained:
      allow = **alw**

LINKED VOWELS

The **'linked vowels'** - **'au'**, **'oa'**, **'oi'**, **'oo'**, **'ou'**, **'ui'** are replaced by **'w'**; any other vowels are deleted with the exception of the **commencing** vowel:-

Examples:-   abr<u>oa</u>d = **abrwd**   br<u>oa</u>d = **brwd**
                 am<u>ou</u>nt = **amwnt**   m<u>ou</u>nt = **mwnt**

EXERCISE 1
Replace the 'linked vowels' 'eu' by 'w' and delete any other vowels.

sl<u>eu</u>th, n<u>eu</u>tral, n<u>eu</u>trality

EXERCISE 2
Replace the 'linked vowels' 'au' by 'w' deleting any other vowels apart from the commencing vowel.
Suffix - **'ing = g'**
*No double letters

appl<u>au</u>d, appl<u>au</u>d/ing, appl<u>au</u>se*,d<u>au</u>nt/ing, f<u>au</u>lt, f<u>au</u>lty, g<u>au</u>nt. g<u>au</u>ntlet, h<u>au</u>l, h<u>au</u>led, h<u>au</u>l/ing, h<u>au</u>nt, h<u>au</u>nted, j<u>au</u>nt, l<u>au</u>dable, p<u>au</u>se*, p<u>au</u>s/ing, sq<u>ua</u>d, sq<u>ua</u>dron, t<u>au</u>nt, t<u>au</u>nted, v<u>au</u>lt, v<u>au</u>lt/ing

*When **'s'** ends a word it changes to **'z'**.
*Exception: 'fault<u>less</u> = **fwltls**', 'less = **ls**'

EXERCISE 3
Replace the 'linked vowels' 'oa' by 'w', deleting any other vowels with the exception of the **commencing vowel.**
Suffix - **'ing = g'**

appr<u>oa</u>ch, appr<u>oa</u>ch/ing, abr<u>oa</u>d, br<u>oa</u>d, br<u>oa</u>den, br<u>oa</u>den/ing, br<u>oa</u>ch, cl<u>oa</u>k, c<u>oa</u>st, c<u>oa</u>stal, g<u>oa</u>l, goat, gr<u>oa</u>n, gr<u>oa</u>n/ing, l<u>oa</u>d, l<u>oa</u>d/ing, l<u>oa</u>n, l<u>oa</u>n/ing, l<u>oa</u>th, l<u>oa</u>thsome, m<u>oa</u>n, m<u>oa</u>t, p<u>oa</u>ch, r<u>oa</u>m, r<u>oa</u>m/ing.

N.B. roast = **rost**, toast = **tost**

EXERCISE 4

Replace the 'linked vowels' 'oi' by 'w'; any other vowels apart from the **commencing vowel** are deleted.
Suffix - **'ing = g'**

avoid, avoided, avoid/ing, boil, boiler, boil/ing, coil, foist, hoist, hoist/ing, memoir, moist, point, pointed, point/ing, pointless*, reservoir, spoil, toil, toil/ing, turmoil, void, void/ing

EXERCISE 5

Replace the 'linked vowels' 'oo' by 'w'; any other vowels apart from the **commencing vowel** are deleted.
Suffix - **'ing = g'**

book, booked, book/ing, boot, broom, cook, cooker, cook/ing, cool, cooler, cool/ing, crook, crooked, fool, foolish, foot, groove, hood, hook, hoot, look, look/ing, loot, loot/ing, moon, noon, pool, proof, rook, scooter, shook, shoot, shoot/ing, tool, tooth

EXERCISE 6

Replace the 'linked vowels' 'ou' by 'w'; any other vowels apart from the commencing vowel are deleted.
Suffix - **'ing = g'**

abound, account, account/ing, amount, amounted, amount/ing, blouse*, bound, boundary, bound/ing, bounty, bounce*, bounced*, bounc/ing, **com**/pound*, count, counter, count/ing, crouch, crouched, crouch/ing, foul, found, ground, grounded, hound, house*, loud, mound, mouth, poultry, pouch, pound, pour, proud, round, recoup, route, routine, scout, shout, surmount, surround, spout, sprout, sprout/ing, stout, trouble, troublesome, trout, vouch, voucher, vouch/ing.

*'s' ending a word changes to 'z'
*'com = cm'
*'c' = 'z'

EXERCISE 7

Replace the 'linked vowels' 'ui' by 'w'; any other vowels apart from the **commencing vowel** are deleted.

Suffix: 'ing = g'

cruise*, fruit, suit*, suited*, suitable*, suit/ing*

*When **'s'** ends a word it changes to **'z'**

*When **'s'** is followed by **'w'** ('ui' = w) the 's' changes to **'z'**, **'suit = zwt'**

EXERCISE 8

The combinations **'augh'** and **'ough'** as in the words **'caught'** and **'bought'** are represented by **'aw'**.

Examples:-   caught = **cawt**   bought = **bawt**

Replace the combinations **'augh'** and **'ough'** by **'aw'**, deleting any other vowels.

bought, brought, daughter, draught, fraught, haughty, naughty, sought, slaughter, taught

CHAPTER 9

DIPTHONGS

1.   A **DIPTHONG** is the union of **two vowel sounds** in one syllable, e.g., **'io'** as in the word **'mill<u>io</u>n'**, and **'ui'** as in the word **'r<u>ui</u>n'**.

Where the **first vowel** in a dipthong is **'i' or 'e'**, as in - **'<u>ea</u>'**, **'<u>eou</u>'**, **'<u>ia</u>'**, **'<u>iai</u>'**, **'<u>ie</u>'**, **'<u>io</u>'**, **'<u>iou</u>'**, **<u>iu</u>'**, the dipthong vowels are replaced by **'y'**; any remaining vowels are **deleted**, with the exception of the **commencing vowel** and **'o'** or **'u'**:

    Examples:

Word	Dipthong Vowels	Agiliwriting
delin<u>ea</u>te	**ea** = y	**dlnyt**
pit<u>eou</u>s*	**eou** = y	**ptyz**
med<u>ia</u>te	**ia** = y	**mdyt**
l<u>iai</u>se*	**iai** = y	**lyz**
propr<u>ie</u>tor	**ie** = y	**proprytr**
un<u>io</u>n	**io** = y	**unyn**
ser<u>iou</u>s*	**iou** = y	**sryz**
med<u>iu</u>m	**iu** = y	**mdym**

    *'s' ending a word changes to **'z'**

2.   Where the **first vowel** in a dipthong is '**o**' or '**u**', as in - '**oe**', '**oi**','**ou**', '**ua**', '**ue**', '**ui**', '**uou**', the dipthong vowels are replaced by '**w**'. Any remaining vowels are deleted, with the exception of the **commencing vowel** and '**o**' or '**u**':

Examples:

Word	Dipthong Vowels		Agiliwriting
poem	oe	= w	pwm
devour	ou	= w	dvwr
fluctuate	ua	= w	fluctwt
affluent	ue	= w	aflwnt
ruin	ui	= w	rwn
tempestuous*	uou	= w	tmpstwz

*'s' ending a word changes to '**z**'

Exceptions:

i)   In the words '**associate**' and '**negotiate**', the dipthong '**ia**' is deleted in the terminations '**ciate**' and '**tiate**'; these terminations are represented by '**zt**'.

    asso/**ciate** = **asozt**
    asso/ciat/ing* = **asoztg**
    asso/cia/tion* = **asozn**
    nego/tiate = **ngozt**
    nego/tiat/ing = **ngoztg**
    nego/tia/tion = **ngozn**

*Suffixes: - '**ing = g**' '**tion = zn**'

ii)   Prefix: '**co-op**' = '**cop**'

    co-operate = **coprht**, co-operating = **coprhtg**, co-operation = **coprhzn**, (operate = **oprht**)

iii)   Prefix: '**co-or**' = '**cor**'

    co-ordinate = **cordnht**,
    co-ordinating = **cordnhtg**,
    co-ordination = **cordnhzn**

iv)   **Prefix: 'rea = ry'**

rea/ppeal = **rypl**	(appeal = **apl**)
rea/rise = **ryrz**	(rise = **rz**)
rea/sses = **ryzs**	(assess = **azs**)

EXERCISES:

Where the **first vowel in a dipthong is either 'e' or 'i'**, the dipthong vowels are replaced by **'y'**; any remaining vowels are **deleted** with the exception of the **commencing vowel** and **'o'** or **'u'**:-

EXERCISE 1.
Retain the **commencing vowel** and replace the **dipthong vowels by 'y'**; any other vowels are deleted with the exception of **'o'** or **'u'**.
*Remember - no double letters.

'ing = g', 'tion = zn'
abbrev **ia** te, abbrev **ia** t ing, affil **ia** te,
affil **ia** tion, allev **ia** te, allev **ia** tion,
approp **ia** tion (retain vowel 'o'),
approp **ia** ting, apprec **ia** te ('c' = 'z'),
apprec **ia** tion, ('c' = 'z')
acqu **ie** sce ('cqu = q','sc = z')

EXERCISE 2.
Replace the **dipthong vowels by 'y'**; any other vowels are **deleted** with the exception of **'o'** or **'u'**:
*No double letters.

bill **io** n, bun **io** n (retain vowel 'u')

EXERCISE 3.
Replace the **dipthong vowels by 'y'**; any other vowels are deleted with the exception of **'o'** or **'u'**:
*No double letters.

'com = cm, 'con = cn'
'ing = g', 'tion = zn'

compan **io** n, compl **ia** nce ('c' = 'z'),
concill **ia** te ('c' = 'z'),conven **ie** nt, conviv **ia** l
cr **ea** te, cr **ea** tion, cr **ea** ting

EXERCISE 4.

Replace the **dipthong vowels by 'y'**; any other vowels are **deleted** with the exception of **'o'** or **'u'**:

'ing = g', 'tion = zn'
's' at the end of a word changes to 'z'.

d **ia** l, d **ia** ry, def **ia** nt, delin **ia** te,
delir **iou** s̲ ('s' changes to **'z'**), deleter **iou** s̲,
dev **iou** s̲, dev **ia** te, dev **ia** tion

Retain the vowel **'u' = 'w'**:-
d u̲b **iou** s̲ ('s' changes to **'z'**)

EXERCISE 5.

Replace the **dipthong vowels by 'y'**; any other vowels are **deleted**.

'ex = x'
e̲x̲ter **io** r, e̲x̲ped **ie** nt, e̲x̲per **ie** n c̲e ('c' changes to **'z'**), e̲x̲ped **ie** nt

Retain the **commencing vowel** and replace the **dipthong vowels by 'y'**; any other vowels are **deleted**:

egalitar **ia** n, e q̲u̲ilibr **iu** m ('qu' = **'q'**)

EXERCISE 6

Replace the **dipthong vowels with 'y'**; any other vowels are deleted with the exception of **'o'** or **'u'**:

famil **ia** r, f o̲l **ia** g e (retain vowel 'o'),
(soft 'g' = **'j'**)

EXERCISE 7

Replace the **dipthong vowels by 'y'**; any other vowels are deleted:

gen **ia** l (soft 'g' = **'j'**), gen **iu** s̲ ('s' changes to **'z'**), ger **ia** tric (soft 'g' = 'j'), gregar **iou** s̲
('s' changes to 'z').

EXERCISE 8

Replace the **dipthong vowels by 'y'**; any other vowels are **deleted**:

hilar **iou** s ('s' changes to 'z'), hes̲s̲ **ia** n ('ss' =   'z'), histr **io** nic

Retain the vowel **'u'** = **'w'**. Replace the **dipthong vowels by 'y'**; any other vowels are deleted:

hercu̱l **ia** n

EXERCISE 9

Replace the **dipthong vowels by 'y'**; any other vowels are **deleted**:

'in = n', 'inex = nx', 'incon = ncn'
'im' before a consonant = **'m'**.

i̱mperv **iou** s̲ ('s' changes to **'z'**),   i̱nexper **ie** n̲c̲e
('c' changes to **'z'**), i̱nconven **ie** n̲c̲e, i̱nfer **io** r,
i̱njur **iou** s̲ ('jur' = **'jr'**), i̱nter **io** r
i̱nstantan **eou** s̲ ('s' changes to 'z'), i̱nvid **iou** s̲

Retain the **commencing vowel 'i'** = **'i'** and replace the **dipthong vowels by 'y'**; any other vowels are **deleted**:

id **ea** l, id **io** t, i d **io** matic, id **iu** m

Retain the   **commencing vowel 'i'** = **'i'**   and the vowel 'o' and replace the dipthong vowels by 'y'; any other vowels are **deleted:**

igno̱min **iou** s̲ (**'s'** = **'z'**)

Retain the **commencing vowel 'i'** = **'i'**, the vowel **'u'** = **'u'** and replace the **dipthong vowels by 'y'**:

illu̱str **iou** s̲ ('s' changes to 'z')

Retain the **commencing vowel 'i'** = **'i'**. Replace the **dipthong vowels by 'y'**; any other vowels are deleted:

i̱mmed **ia** te, immed **ia** tely

EXERCISE 10

The vowel **'o' is retained**. Replace the **dipthong vowels by 'y'**; any other vowels are deleted:

jo̱v **ia** l,   Jaco̱b **ea** n

EXERCISE 11
Replace the **dipthong vowels by 'y'**; any other vowels are deleted:

l **ia** ble, l **iai** s̲e ('s' changes to **'z'**), l **ia** s̲on̲ ('son = **zn**')

EXERCISE 12
Replace the **dipthong vowels by 'y'**; any other vowels are **deleted**:

med **ia** l med **ia** te, med **ia** t̲i̲o̲n̲ (tion = zn),
med **io** cre, med **io** crity, med **iu** m, mill **io** n, my̲ster **iou** s̲ (delete **'y'**, 's' = **'z'**),
mis̲c̲ellan **eou** s̲ ('sc' = **'z'**, 's' = **'z'**),
mater **ia** l, mater **ia** listic

EXERCISE 13
Replace dipthong vowels by **'y'** and retain the first vowel **'o'**.

no̲tor **ie** ty, no̲tor **iou** s̲   ('s' = **'z'**)

Retain the vowel **'u' = 'w'**. Replace the **dipthong vowels by 'y'**:

nu̲tr **ie** nt

EXERCISE 14
Retain the **commencing vowel 'o'**. Replace the **dipthong vowels by 'y'**; any other vowels are deleted:

obed **ie** nt, obv **iou** s̲ ('s' changes to **'z'**),
obv **ia** te, obv **ia** t̲i̲o̲n̲ (tion = **zn**), on **io** n,
or **ie** nt, or **ie** ntal.

EXERCISE 15
Replace the **dipthong vowels by 'y'**; any other vowels are **deleted**:

p **iou** s̲ ('s' changes to **'z'**),   p **ia** nist, prem **iu** m,
prev **iou** s̲ ('s' changes to **'z'**), pr **io** r

EXERCISE 16

Retain the vowel **'o'**. Replace the **dipthong vowels by 'y'**; any other vowels are **deleted:**

pr<u>o</u>verb **ia** l, pr<u>o</u>pr **ie** tor, p **ia** no

EXERCISE 17

Replace the **dipthong vowels by 'y'**; any other vowels are **deleted**:

r **ea** l, r **ea** listic, rebell **iou** <u>s</u> ('s' changes to **'z'**), rel **ia** ble, retal **ia** te, retal **ia** <u>ting</u> ('ing = **g'**) retal **ia** <u>tion</u> (tion = **zn**) remed **ia** l

EXERCISE 18

Replace the **dipthong vowels by 'y'**; any other vowels are **deleted**:

ser **ia** l, secretar **ia** l, ser **iou** <u>s</u> ('s' changes to **'z'**), sc **ie** ntific ('sc' = **'s'**)

Retain the vowel **'o'**. Replace the **dipthong vowels by 'y'**; any other vowels are deleted:

sp<u>o</u>ntan **eou** <u>s</u> ('s' changes to **'z'**)

EXERCISE 19

Replace the **dipthong vowels by 'y'**; any other vowels are **deleted:**

ted **iou** <u>s</u> ('s' changes to 'z'), th **ea** tre,
th **ea** trical, tr **ia** l

EXERCISE 20

Retain the commencing vowel **'u'** = **'u'**. Replace the dipthong vowels by **'y'**:-

un **io** n

EXERCISE 21

Replace the dipthong vowels by **'y'**; any other vowels are deleted:-

v **ia** ble, v **io** lin, v **io** linist, vitr **io** lic

EXERCISE 22
Copy the following examples:

i)   The terminations **'ciate'** and **'tiate'** = **'zyt'**:

appre/**ciate** = **aprzyt**
de/pre/**ciate** = **dprzyt**
sub̲stan/**tiate** = **sbstnzyt**   ('sub = **sb**')

ii)   **'geo'** = **'jy'** - **the soft sound of 'g' = 'j'.**

geo/logy = **jyljy**   ('logy = **ljy**')
geo/graphy = **jygrfy** ('graphy = **grfy**')

iii)   The vowel **'a'** is retained following **'r'**:-

rad **ia** nt = **radynt**
rad ia tor = **radytr**   ('tor = **tr**')
ex̲tran eou s̲ = **xtranyz**   ('**ex** = **x**')

iv)   **'ran = rhn'**

mediterran **ea** n = **mdtrhnyn**
sub̲terra̲nean = **sbtrhnyn** ('sub' = **sb**)

EXERCISES
Where the **first vowel in a dipthong is 'o'** or **'u'** - the dipthong vowels are
replaced by **'w'**; any remaining vowels are deleted with the exception of the
commencing vowel and the vowels **'o'** or **'u'**.

EXERCISE 23
Retain the **commencing vowel 'a'** and **replace the dipthong vowels by**
'w'; any other vowels are deleted.
*No double letters.

affl **ue** nt, atten **ua** te, act **ua** l,
act **ua** ry, act **ua** r **ia** l ('ia' = **'y'**),
ac **ui** ty, accent **ua** te ('accent = **acsnt**'),
accent **ua** tio̲n ('tion = **zn**'), ambig **uou** s̲ ('s' changes to **'z'**)

EXERCISE 24
Replace the **dipthong vowels by 'w'**; any other vowels are deleted:

'con = cn'
c **oi** n, c **oi** ncide ('cide = sd'), <u>con</u>tig uou <u>s</u>
('s' changes to **'z'**), <u>con</u>tin **uou** <u>s</u>, <u>con</u>tin **ua** l,
<u>con</u>tin **ua** <u>tion</u>, <u>con</u>tempt **uou** <u>s</u>, cr **ue** l, cr **ue** lty

EXERCISE 25
Retain the **commencing vowel** and replace the **dipthong vowels by 'w'**; any other vowels are **deleted**:

'tion = zn'
eval **ua** te, eval **ua** <u>tion</u>, <u>ex</u>ten **ua** te, <u>ex</u>ten **ua** <u>tion</u>

EXERCISE 26
Replace the **dipthong vowels by 'w'**; any other vowels are **deleted** with the exception of **'o' or 'u'**:

'ing = g', 'tion = zn'
fl<u>u</u>ct **ua** te ('u' = **'u'**), fl<u>u</u>ct **ua** <u>ting</u>,
fl<u>u</u>ct **ua** <u>tion</u>, fl ui d, fl ue nt

EXERCISE 27
Replace the **dipthong vowels by 'w'**; any other vowels are deleted:

her **oi** c, her **oi** sm

EXERCISE 28
'im = m before a consonant'
'in = n' 'incon = ncn'
'cial = zl'

<u>im</u>pet **uou** <u>s</u> ('s' changes to **'z'**),<u>incon</u>spic **uou** <u>s</u>, <u>in</u>fl **ue** n<u>c</u>e ('c' = **'s'**), <u>in</u>fl **ue** ntial 'cial = **zl'**),
<u>in</u>tellect **ua** l

EXERCISE 29

Replace the **dipthong vowels by 'w'**; any other vowels are **deleted** with the exception of **'o'** or **'u'**:

perpet **ua** l, perspic **uou** s̲ ('s' changes to **'z'**), p **oe** t, p **oe** try, p **oe** m, pu̲nct **ua** l̲ (u = **u**)

EXERCISE 30

Replace the **dipthong vowels by 'w'**; any other vowels are deleted:

r **ui** n, r **ui** nous ('nous = **nz'**), r **ui** nation
('nation = **nhzn'**)

EXERCISE 31

Replace the dipthong vowels by 'w'; any other vowels are deleted:

ten **uou** s̲ ('s' changes to **'z'**), tempest **uou** s̲,

EXERCISE 32

Replace the **dipthong vowels by 'w'**; any other vowels are **deleted** with the exception of **'o' or 'u'**:

virt **ua** l, virt **uou** s̲ ('s' changes to **'z'**), virt **uo** so̲

N.B.
i)   's' changes to 'z' when followed by **'w':**
     s **ui** cide = **zwsd** (cide = **sd**)
ii) bi̲ling **ua** l = **bylngwl (bi = by)**

CHAPTER 10

THE VOWEL 'i'

The phonetics applicable to the Vowel 'i'.

The vowel 'i' has two different sounds; the **short-hard** sound of 'i' as in the word 'bit' and the **long-soft** sound of 'i' as in the word 'bite'.

1.   Words containing the **short-hard** sound of 'i' - the 'i' remains unchanged.

bit = bit

2.   Words containing the **long-soft** sound of 'i' - the 'i' is represented by '**y**'.

bite = byt

3.   Words **commencing** with 'i' - the 'i' remains unchanged.

item = itm

Where the **long-soft** sound of 'i' is linked to a **silent vowel and/or silent consonant(s)**, as in the combinations - **'eigh', 'ie', 'igh', 'ui'**, the combinations are represented by '**y**': any remaining vowels are deleted with the exception of the **commencing vowel**.

> applied = **aplyd,** flight = **flyt**
> guide = **gyd,** height = **hyt**
> while = **wyl*,** ryhme = **rym***

* Silent consonant '**h**' is deleted.

EXERCISE 1.

Abbreviate the following words, retaining the **short-hard** sound of 'i' as 'i', deleting any other vowels.

Examples: bit = **bit**   bitter = **bitr**

(chip), chipped, chipp/ing*, differ, (dip), dipped, dipp/ing, (dig), digg/ing*, (fit), fitted, fitt/ing, (lift), lifted, lift/ing*, (rip), ripped, ripp/ing*, (tip), tipped, tipping.

*No double letters
*'ing = g'

EXERCISE 2.

Abbreviate the following words, replacing the **long-soft sound of 'i' by 'y'** and deleting any other vowels, apart from the **commencing vowel.**

Examples:

bide = **byd,** abide = **abyd**, abided = **abydd,** abiding = **abydg**

a**wh**ile*, bile, bite, bit/ing, bridal, bride, com/pile*, con/trite*, dine, din/ing, fine, fire, hire, ig/nite, line, liner, mine, nine, pie, pile, pipe, rhyme, ride, rife, rifle, spire, spite, strife, strike, stripe, tide, tie, time, tripe, trite, unite, unit/ing, strife, strike, stripe, tithe, title, tribal, tribe, vile, w**h**ile, wide, widen, widen/ing, wife, wine.

*silent 'h' is deleted
*'com = cm', 'con = cn'
*Suffix - 'ing = g'

EXERCISE 3.

Abbreviate the following words, retaining the **commencing** vowel 'i' as 'i' and deleting any other vowels.

Examples: ill = **il**   item = itm

i**c**e*, i**c**icle, idle, irrespective*

*No double letters
*Replace 'c' by 'z'

EXERCISE 4.
Abbreviate the following words, replacing the - **combinations** - **'eigh'**, **'ie'**, **'igh'**, **'ui'**, by **'y'**; any other vowels are deleted, with the exception of the **commencing** vowel:-

allied, alight/ing, applied, *acquire, bright, brighten, com/plied*, die, died, denied, fight, fight/ing, fried, fright, guile, guid/ing, height, lied, lie/ing, light, lighted, light/ing, mighty, night, pie, plight, relied, replied, right, tie, tight, tighten, tighten/ing.

*'acq = aq'
*'com = cm'
*Suffix - 'ing = g'

EXERCISE 5
Copy the following examples; **'ie'** is replaced by **'y'** in plurals:-

discrepancies = **dscrpnzys** (c = z), families = **fmlys**, irregularities = **irglrtys**, remedies = **rmdys**

Exceptions:
i)   The combination **'ie'** is deleted in the termination **'fied = fd'**.
     e.g. 'identi**fied** = **idntfd**', 'recti**fied** = **rctfd**'.

ii) The combination **'ui'** is deleted in the termination **'quire = qr'**.
     e.g. 'ac**quire** = **aqr**', 're**quire** = **rqr**'.

iii) Where the prefix **'im'** is followed by a consonant, **'im = m'**.
     e.g. '**im**ply = **mply**' '**im**plicit = **mplzt**'.

iv) The prefix - **'in = n'**
     e.g. '**in**stant = **nstnt**', '**in**side = **nsd**'.

v)   The termination **'ise = z'**.
     e.g. 'minim**ise** = **mnmz**', 'subsid**ise** = **sbsdz**'.

vi) The termination - **'scribe = scrb'**.
     e.g. 'a**scribe** = **ascrb**', 'de**scribe** = **dscrb**'.

vii) **Shorts** - all vowels are deleted.
     e.g. *'bill = bl', 'like = lk', 'side = sd'*, etc.

CHAPTER 11

Allan

THE VOWEL 'u'

THE 'PHONETICS' applicable to the VOWEL 'u'.

The vowel 'u' has **two different sounds** - the **short-hard** sound of **'u'** as in the word **'tub'** and, the **long-soft sound** of **'u'** as in the word **'tube'**.

1. Words containing the **short-hard sound** of **'u'** the **'u'** remains unchanged.

    tub = **tub**

2. Words containing the **long-soft sound** of **'u'** the **'u'** is represented by **'w'**.

    tube = **twb**

3. Words commencing with **'u'** the **'u'** remains unchanged.

    under = **undr**

*Remember, that **'u'** is the **highest vowel** in the phonetic scale - all other vowels are deleted.

EXERCISE 1.
   Abbreviate the following words, retaining the **short-hard** sound of **'u'** as **'u'**; any other vowels are deleted, with the exception of the **commencing vowel:**

Example: abUndant = **abUndnt**

   AnnUl, bUffer, bUndle, bUtton, bUtter, cUtter, destrUctive, dUster, fUndamental, fUrrow, gUnner, hUddle, hUnger, hUnter, jUggle, lUmber, mUddle, mUltiple, mUtton, nUll, pUlpit, pUnter, redUndant, rUbber, rUmple, rUstic, sUffer, sUffix, sUmmary, sUmmer, sUmmon, trUndle, trUsted, tUnnel, vUlgar, vUlnerable.

EXERCISE 2.
   Abbreviate the following words, replacing the **long-soft sound** of **'u'** by **'w'**; any other vowels are deleted, with the exception of the **commencing vowel:**

Example: acute = **acwt**   cute = **cwt**

   AbUse*, AcUse*, AmUse*, brUte, brUtal, bUgle, compUte, compUter, crUde, cUbe, cUbicle, fUgitive*, fUse*, fUtile, fUtility, hUman, hUman-ity, jUvenile, lUbricate, mUle, mUte, *refUse, refUte, rUde, rUle, rUse*, sprUce*.
*'s' = 'z'
*'c' = 'z'
*soft 'g' = 'j'

EXERCISE 3.
   Abbreviate the following words, retaining the commencing vowel **'u'** as **'u'**; any other vowels are deleted:

   Examples: under = **under**   utensil = **utnsl**

   Ultimate, Understand, Unless*, Umbilical, Umpire, Utter, Utility, Usurper, Universe,* Universal,* University*, Use*
*'s' = 'z'
* less = **ls**

*Remember - no double letters.

Exceptions

The vowel **'u'** is deleted in the following syllables:

'bur = br'
e.g. 'burden = **brdn**', 'bursar = **brsr**'

'fur = fr'
e.g. 'furnish = **frnsh**', 'further = **frthr**'

'hur = hr'
e.g. 'hurdle = **hrdl**'

'mur = mr'
e.g. 'murder = **mrdr**', 'murmer = **mrmr**'

'sur = sr'
e.g. 'surprise = **srprz**', 'surface* = **srfs**'
(face = **fs**)

CHAPTER 12

LINKED CONSONANTS

LINKED CONSONANTS are as follows:-

bl, br, ch, chr, cl, cr, dr, fl, fr, gl, gr, kl, kn, kr, pl, ph, pr, sc, sch, scr, sh, sl, sm, sn, sp, spr, st, str, sw, th, tr, wh.

Words holding **'linked consonants'** cannot conform to the phonetic scale applicable to the deletion of the vowels.

By removing the vowel lying between **'linked consonants'** in the **first syllable** of the words shown below, another word results:

Word	*Syllables*	*Longhand*
below	be/low	**blow**
sallow	sal/low	**slow**
follow	fol/low	**flow**
borrow	bor/row	**brow**
derive	de/rive	**drive**
palace	pa/lace	**place**
sewing	se/wing	**swing**
terrace	ter/race	**trace**

Agiliwriting deals with words commencing with 'linked consonants' in the following ways:

1.   Where the vowel **'a'** lies either side of **'l'** or **'r'** as in - **'ala'** and **'ara'**, the vowel **'a'** **in the first syllable is deleted** and the **second vowel 'a' is replaced by 'h'** as shown in the examples below:

ballast	bal/last = blhst	(blast = blast)
palace	pa/lace = plhz	(place = plaz)
embarrass	em/bar/rass = mbrhz	(mbrace = mbraz)

*'para = prh':

paragraph	**para**/graph = **prhgrf**	(graph = grf)
parade	**para**/de = **prhd**	
parallel	**para**/llel = **prhll**	
parasite*	**para**/site = **prhsyt**	(site = syt)
paramount	**para**/mount = **prhmwnt**	(mount = mwnt)
separate	se/**para**/te = **sprht**	
com/parable	com/**para**/ble = **cmprhbl**	(com = cm)
com/parative	com/**para**/tive = **cmprhtv**	(com = cm)
ap/paratus	a/**para**/tus = **aprhtz**	

Exceptions:
   Shorts - all vowels are deleted:
   'balance = blnz', *'character = crctr'*.

2)   Where words in this category contain the terminations - **'late'** and **'rate'**; the consonant **'h'** replaces the vowel **'a'** following the consonants **'l'** and **'r'**; **all other vowels are deleted.**

Terminations:
   'late = lht', 'lating = lhtg', 'lation = lhzn'
   'rate = rht', 'rating = rhtg', 'ration = rhzn'.

Linked Consonants - 'c - l' (cl)
   calculate = **clclht**
   calculating = **clclhtg**
   calculation = **clclhzn**

   collate   = **clht**
   collating = **clhtg**
   collation = **clhzn**

Linked Consonants: 'g - l' (gl)
regu<u>late</u> = **rglht**
regu<u>lating</u> = **rglhtg**
regu<u>lation</u> = **rglhzn**

Linked Consonants: 'p - r' (pr)
ope<u>rate</u> - **oprht**
ope<u>rating</u> = **oprhtg**
ope<u>ration</u> = **oprhzn**

Linked Consonants: 'c - r' (cr), 'p - r' (pr)
corpo<u>rate</u> = **crprht**
corpo<u>ration</u> = **crprhzn**

Linked Consonants: 'c - r' (cr), 'b - r' (br)
corrobo<u>rate</u>* = **crobrht**
corrobo<u>rating</u> = **crobrhtg**
corrobo<u>ration</u> = **crobrhzn**
*'corro = cro'

Linked Consonants: 'b - r' (br), 'd - r' (dr),
    't - r'(tr)
reverbe<u>rate</u> = **rvrbrht**
conside<u>rate</u> = **cnsdrht**
illi<u>terate</u> = **iltrht**
obli<u>terate</u> = **obltrht**

3. Where the **vowel 'a'** lies in the **first syllable** followed by either **'e' or 'i'** (these vowels are lower in the phonetic scale than the vowel **'a'**) all the vowels **'e'** or **'i'** are **deleted**, and the vowel **'a'** in the first syllable of the word is replaced by **'h'**.
    *No double letters

Word	_Syllables_	_Agiliwriting_	_Linked Consonants_
b<u>a</u>llet	b<u>a</u>l/let	**bhly**	**bl**
b<u>a</u>rrel	b<u>a</u>r/rel	**bhrl**	**br**
b<u>a</u>rren	b<u>a</u>r/ren	**bhrn**	**br**
b<u>a</u>llistic	b<u>a</u>l/lis/tic	**bhlstc**	**bl**
b<u>a</u>rrister	b<u>a</u>r/ri/ster	**bhrstr**	**br**

4.   Where words terminate in - **'low' and 'row'**, the vowel lying in the first syllable is retained:

'low = lw', 'row = rw'

sallow = **salw**   (sl)
borrow = **borw**   (br)
follow = **folw**   (fl)
Exception:
'Short' : **'below = blw'**

5.   The rule applicable to other words in this category is that the **vowel lying in the first syllable of the word is deleted** and the **vowel lying in the second syllable of the word is retained**:

*The vowel **'e'** is deleted in the first syllable and the consonant **'h'** replaces the vowel 'a' in the second syllable:

terrace   ter/race = **trhz**   (trace = traz)

* **'col = cl'**
The vowel **'o'** in the first syllable is **deleted. The vowel 'i' in the second syllable is retained**; any other vowels are **deleted**.

col/lide   = **clyd***
col/lude   = **clwd**
col/lu<u>sion</u> = **clwzn**   ('sion = zn')

*The **long-soft** sound of **'i' = 'y'**
*The **long-soft** sound of **'u' = 'w'**

* The vowel **'o'** in the first syllable is **deleted. The vowel 'a' in the second syllable is retained**; any other vowels are **deleted**.

col/lapse*   = **clapz**
col/laps/ing = **clapzg** (suffix 'ing = g')
col/lapsible = **clapzbl**

*The 'root word' is **'lap = lap', 'lapse = lapz'**, and this form of 'a' is retained.

*   The vowel **'o'** in the first syllable is **deleted**. The vowel **'o'** in the second syllable is **retained**:-

    col/ony = **clony**
    col/onial = **clonyl**
    col/loquial = **cloqyl**   (qu = q)
    co/lossal = **clozl**   (ss = z)

*   **'cor = cr'**
The vowel **'o'** in the first syllable is **deleted**. **The vowel 'o' in the second syllable is retained;** any other vowels are **deleted:**
*No double letters

    cor/rode   = **crod**
    cor/rod/ing = **crodg**   (ing = g)
    cor/ro/sion = **crozn**   (sion = zn)

* **'cor=cr' (cr)**
The **vowel in the first syllable is deleted.**
The vowel **'u'** in the **second syllable is retained**:

    cor/rupt = **crupt**
    cor/rupt/ing = **cruptg**
    cor/rup/<u>tion</u>* = **crupn***

*(**'tion' following 'p' = 'n'**)

* The **vowel in the first syllable is deleted.**
The vowel **'o'** in the **second syllable is retained**:-

    b-r (br), f-l (fl), f-r (fr), t-r (tr).

    ba/ro/meter = **bromtr**
    fe/lony = **flony**
    fe/ro/cious = **froshz**   ('cious = shz')
    ter/ror = **tror**
    ter/ro/rise = **trorz**   ('rise = rz')

*The **vowel in the first syllable is deleted;** the vowel **'u'**, in the second syllable is retained:
The **long-soft sound** of the vowel **'u' = 'w'.**
Where **'s'** is followed by **'w'**, **'s' changes to 'z'**:

      *'sal = zl'
      salute   = **zlwt**
      salutation = **zlwtzn**   ('tation = tzn')

      * **'sol' = 'zl'**
      so/luble = **zlwbl**
      so/lu/tion = **zlwzn**   ('tion = zn')
      re/solution = **rzlwzn**

* 'absolute = **abzlwt**'

* s - t = **'zt'**
The **vowel in the first syllable is deleted.**
The dipthong **'ua = w'** in the second syllable is **retained:**

      situate = **ztwt**
      situat/ing = **ztwtg**   ('ing = g')
      situa/tion = **ztwzn**   ('tion = zn')

* t - r = **'tr'**
The highest vowel **'o'** is retained; any other vowels are deleted:

      territory = **trtory**
      territorial = **trtoryl**   (dipthong **'ia' = 'y'**)

*All vowels are **deleted** in the following words, **where words of more than two syllables hold the short-hard vowels 'e' and/or 'i'**:

      terrible = **trbl**
      terrify = **trfy**
      terrific = **trfc**

* **'d-r' (dr), 's-l' (sl), 's-p' (sp)**

      derive = **drv**
      solicitor = **slztr**   **('Short')**
      suppose = **spz**   **('Short')**
      supply = **sply**   **('Short')**

* **'s-m' (zm)**

      similar = **zmlr**
      dis/similar = **dzmlr**

CHAPTER 13

CONSONANT 'H'

1. The **consonant 'h'** is used to represent the **long-sound** of 'a', 'ai'; thus:-

long-soft sound	*short-hard sound*
b<u>ai</u>l = **bhl**	(ball = **bal**)
f<u>a</u>te = **fht**	(fat = **fat**)
f<u>ai</u>l = **fhl**	(fall = **fal**)
l<u>ai</u>d = **lhd**	(lad = **lad**)
r<u>ai</u>n = **rhn**	(ran = **ran**)

2. The consonant **'h' replaces the vowel 'a'** in the following terminations; **any other vowels are deleted** with the exception of the commencing vowel:-

$$
\begin{aligned}
\text{l\underline{a}te} &= \textbf{lht} \\
\text{rel\underline{a}te} &= \textbf{rlht} \\
\text{nate} &= \textbf{nht} \\
\text{termin\underline{a}te} &= \textbf{trmnht} \\
\text{r\underline{a}te} &= \textbf{rht} \\
\text{operate} &= \textbf{oprht}
\end{aligned}
$$

3.   The consonant **'h'** cannot replace the vowel **'a'** when this vowel follows
      the consonants **- c, p, s, t,** as, **'ch', 'ph', 'sh', 'th',** would result.
      When the **long-soft vowels 'a'** or, **'ai'** follow these consonants, they are
      either, deleted or retained:

cape = **cap***	chase = **chaz**
share = **shr** ('Short')	hair = **har**

* *Not applicable to 'Agilityping'.*

4.   **Agiliwriting**
      Where differently spelt words, having identical abbreviations, are used in
      Agiliwriting, these can be transcribed back into their longhand forms
      according to the context in which they appear. For e.g.:

      Where the **long-soft vowels 'ee'** or **'ea'** occur between consonants, the
      vowels are **completely deleted**; there are also **'Shorts'** which produce the
      same abbreviation.

'Shorts'	*Long-Soft Vowels*
and = **nd**	n<u>ee</u>d = **nd**
did = **dd**	d<u>ee</u>d = **dd**
fill = **fl**	f<u>ee</u>l = **fl**
her = **hr**	h<u>ea</u>r = **hr**
were = **wr**	w<u>ea</u>r = **wr**

Agilityping
Each abbreviation has to be different so that the computer can identify **differently spelt words** for automatic transcription into their **longhand form.**

An **'h'** is attached to differentiate between these identical abbreviations and
follows words holding the **long-soft vowels** of **'ee' and ea'** as shown below:-

Agilityping
      need = **ndh**, deed = **ddh**, feel = **flh**, hear = **hrh**, wear = **wrh**

*Exception:
here = hre

* *The **Agilityping** forms can also be used in **Agiliwriting**.*

CHAPTER 14

'S' REVERSIBLE

AGILIWRITING
Where **differently spelt words** have **identical shorthand abbreviations**, these can be transcribed back into their longhand forms according to the context in which they appear.

AGILITYPING
Where automatic transcription into full English language is required using **Agilityping software**, each abbreviation has to be **different**. Thus, where words contain different vowels lying between identical consonants,* the consonant **'s'** changes to **'z'** in some words, enabling the **Agilityping** programme to identify different spellings:

Examples:

's'		'z'	
advice*	= **advs**	advise	= **advz**
serial	= **sryl**	cereal*	= **zryl**
decent*	= **dsnt**	descent*	= **dznt**
site	= **syt**	cite	= **zyt**
list	= **lst**	last	= **lzt**
lose	= **lws**	loose	= **lwz**

* The soft sound of **'c'** = **'s'**

is = **s**	see = **z**
recent* = **rsnt**	resent = **rznt**
sample = **smpl**	simple = **zmpl**
sell = **sl**	sale = **zl**
seat = **st**	set = **zt**
sold = **sold**	solid = **zold**
soon = **sn**	seen = **zn**
since = **snz**	sense = **znz**
still = **stl**	settle = **ztl**
smaller = **smlr**	similar = **zmlr**
sport = **sport**	support = **zport**
principal = **prnspl**	principle = **prnzpl**

3.   When the consonant 's' **ends** a word, it changes to 'z'. The consonant 's' **then follows 'z' to indicate plurals.**

Examples:-

close = **cloz**	closes = **clozs**
dress = **drz**	dresses = **drzs**
house = **hwz**	houses = **hwzs**

* **Dipthong 'ea = y'**

CHAPTER 15

Allan **CONSONANT 'Y'**

1) AGILIWRITING

According to the **Agiliwriting** principles of abbreviation, the **long-soft** sounds of **'i'**, **'ie'** and **'igh'** are represented by **'y'**; any remaining vowels are deleted, as shown below:-

cite	= **syt**	sight	= **syt**	site	= **syt**
right	= **ryt**	write	= **ryt**		
higher	= **hyr**	hire	= **hyr**		
tied	= **tyd**	tide	= **tyd**		

2) AGILITYPING

Where automatic computer transcription into full English language is required using **Agilityping software,** each abbreviation must be **different** so that the computer can identify **differently spelt words:-**

cite	= **zyt**	sight	= **sght**	site	= **syt**
right	= **ryt**	write	= **wrt**		
higher	= **hghr**	hire	= **hyr**		
per	= **pr**	pair	= **prh**		

3)   The **consonant 'y'** is used to represent the **long-soft** sound of **'ea'** in some
      words where it is necessary to indicate the difference between words
      containing **different vowel sounds between identical consonants:**

Examples:

birch = **brch**
breach = **brych**

perch = **prch**
preach = **prych**

birth = **brth**
breath = **bryth**

and = **nd (Short)**
need = **nyd**

repel = **rpl**
repeal = **rpyl**

there = **thr**
their = **thyr**

them = **thm**
theme = **thym**

revel = **rvl**
reveal = **rvyl**

fee = **fe**
fees = **fys**

4)   The consonant **'y'** replaces the vowels **'ie'** in plurals.

economy = **ecnomy**   economies = **ecnomys**
policy = **polzy**   policies = **polzys**
remedy = **rmdy**   remedies = **rmdys**

5)   The consonant **'y'** replaces the **'dipthong'** vowels where the first vowel
      in the dipthong begins with either **'e'** or **'i'**, as in, **'mediate = mdyt'**, and
      'permeate = prmyt', etc. (Refer to chapter on 'Dipthongs').

CHAPTER 16

APOSTROPHIES

1. In some **identical abbreviations**, an **apostrophe** is added to indicate **plurals**:

Examples:-

gentleman*	= **jntlmn**	gentlemen	= **jntlmn'**
policeman*	= **plzmn**	policemen	= **plzmn'**
salesman*	= **zlsmn**	salesmen	= **zlsmn'**
saleswoman	= **zlswmn**	saleswomen	= **zlswmn'**

*Soft 'g' = 'j'
*'police = plz' ('Short')
*'sale = zl' ('Short')

2. **Agiliwriting**
   Where automatic computer transcription is not required, the writer can **translate identical abbreviations according to the context in which they appear**.

Examples:-

attend	= **atnd**	attained	= **atnd**
complement	= **cmplmnt**	compliment	= **cmplmnt**
contend	= **cntnd**	contained	= **cntnd**
load	= **lwd**	loud	= **lwd**
tool	= **twl**	toil	= **twl**
week	= **wk**	weak	= **wk**

*toll = tol'

3. **Agilityping**
   For computer transcription purposes, each abbreviation has to be different. An **apostrophe** is added to enable the computer to identify **different vowels lying between identical consonants**, i.e. **differently spelt words**.

Examples:-

attend	= **atnd**	attained	= **atnd'**
compliment	= **cmplmnt**	complement	= **cmplmnt'**
cool	= **cwl**	coil	= **cwl'**
contained	= **cntnd**	contend	= **cntnd'**
broach	= **brwch**	brooch	= **brwch'**
load	= **lwd**	loud	= **lwd'**
read	= **rd**	road	= **rd'**
spoil	= **spwl**	spool	= **spwl'**
tool	= **twl**	toil	= **twl'**
week	= **wk**	weak	= **wk'**

*Refer to the **Agilityping** dictionary for words in this category.

CHAPTER 17

SHORTS

'**Shorts**' are frequently used words which are easily recognisable in their abbreviated form and can be as short as one character. Words in this category have to be memorised as they do not conform to the rules applicable to the deletion of the vowels, as **apart from the commencing vowel, they hold consonants* only.**

Exceptions:

*'our = ur', 'you = u'

A '**Short**' does not change with the application of a **prefix and/or suffix, or an additional syllable;** with the exception of the commencing vowel, the vowels are deleted throughout.

Examples:

```
cash  = csh
cash/ing  = cshg        ('ing = g')
en/cash/ing  = ncshg    ('en = n', 'ing = g')
en/cash/ment = ncshm    ('ment = m')
cashier  = cshr
```

EXERCISES.

Transcribe the following sentences into **'Shorts'** by **deleting all the vowels**. Where words are **'underlined'**, **copy** the abbreviations given at the foot of the exercises.

Suffix: 'ing = g'
* No double letters

1)   We will be <u>seeing</u> them very soon.
2)   He <u>said</u> he <u>would</u> write to me before the show.
3)   Is there any way we can get <u>their</u> cash boxes to them today?
4)   We <u>saw</u> our friends in Winchester yesterday. They have a very <u>busy</u> <u>business</u> there.
5)   Did <u>you</u> send them the samples they requested?
6)   They are likely to be travell/ing to Japan in September.
7)   We are hop/ing to make the long journey to <u>see</u> <u>our</u> friends in the month of May.
8)   <u>Our</u> customers were very pleased with the goods we delivered to them.
9)   In <u>which</u> country will <u>you</u> be taking <u>your</u> holiday this year?
10) When can you give me a breakdown <u>of</u> the retail figures to be given to the bank?
11) We <u>should</u> be grateful if <u>you</u> <u>could</u> now <u>settle</u> <u>your</u> bill.
12) There are some very cheap goods to be had in the markets.

'Shorts'
seeing = **zg**, said = **zd**, would = **wd**, their = **thyr**, saw = **zw**, busy = **bzy**, business = **bznz**, you = **u**, see = **z**, our = **ur**, which = **wch**, of = **v**, should = **shd**, could = **cd**, settle = **ztl,** your = **y**.

*Answers to these exercises can be found at the end of the book.

CHAPTER 18

STRINGS

'STRINGS' further abbreviate **Agiliwriting** basic shorthand by **stringing together words which occur in frequently used short phrases; or 'strings' together letters to represent strings of words.** The writing or typing of these 'strings' saves time. (There are over **500 variations** in the **'Strings'** dictionary).

Examples:

1. we enclose herewith
    w nclz hwth   BASIC SHORTHAND
    w e h
    weh   STRING

2. we enclose herewith for your attention
    w nclz hwth f y atnzn   BASIC SHORTHAND
    w e h f y atn
    wehfytn   STRING

3. we acknowledge receipt of your letter of
    w aknwlj rzt v y ltr v   BASIC SHORTHAND
    w ak r v y l v
    wakrvylv   STRING

4.   we thank you for your letter of
        w tnk u f y ltr v   **BASIC SHORTHAND**
        w t u f y l v
        wtufylv   **STRING**

5.   we are in receipt of your letter of
        w r n rzt v y ltr v   **BASIC SHORTHAND**
        w r n r v y l v
        wrnrvylv   **STRING**

6.   we thank you for your quotation of
        w tnk u f y qwtn v   **BASIC SHORTHAND**
        w t u f y qt v
        wtufyqtv   **STRING**

7.   with reference to your order no.
        wth rfrnz t y ordr no.   **BASIC SHORTHAND**
         w rf t y o no.
        wrftyono.   **STRING**

Other words are linked together for speed purposes although they retain their
basic shorthand form.

Examples:
        we have been/**whvbn**, we have not been/**whvntbn**, we have not been able/
        whvntbnabl, we are unable/**wrunbl,** etc.

EXERCISES

Read and copy the 'Agiliwriting' shorthand sentences. 'Strings' are *italicised*:-.

1. Dsr,
    Wakrvylv ydysdt nd wwlb wrtg tu agn asns wrabl t gvu th nfmzn* u rqr.
    Yf,
    Scrtry
*Can also be **'nfo'**.

1a. *Dear Sir,*
    We acknowledge receipt of your letter of yesterday's date and *we will be* writing *to you* again *as soon as we are able* to *give you* the information* you require.
    Yours faithfully,
    Secretary

2. Ftnv - Mr Wlym Whnryt
    D Mr Whnryt,
    Asrqbu wehfytn th lsts v itms abwt wch u nqrd.
    Wlkfwd t an nshl ordr wch wl rzv ur prompt nd crfl atnzn.
    Yf,
    Mhl Ordr Dpt

2a. *For attention of* - Mr William Wainwright
    Dear Mr. Wainwright,
    As requested by you, we enclose herewith for your attention the lists of items about which you enquired.
    We look forward to an initial order which will receive our prompt and careful attention.
    Yours faithfully,
    Mail Order *Department*

3. Dsrs,
    Wrgrtnfmu tht dw t unfzn producn dfcltys wrunbl t kp t th promsd dlvdt. Wrdglwcn t rctfy th pzn nd ask u t acpt ur snzrapls f nyncnv czd tu nthsmtr.
    Yf,
    Prodcn Mnjr

3a. *Dear Sirs,*
    We regret to inform you that due to unforeseen production difficulties *we are unable* to keep to the promised delivery date. *We are doing all we can* to rectify the position and ask you to accept our *sincere apologies* for *any inconvenience* caused *to you in this matter*.
    Yours faithfully,
    Production Manager

4.   **Dmdm,**
      Nacdwyrq whv sntu undr sprht cvr ur patrn bwk v armchr cvrs f y
      slcn.
      Wlkfwd t rzvg y ordr wch wlhv ur imdatn.
      Yf,
      Fbhfv
      Gloryz Frnshg Mtryls Lmtd

4a.   *Dear Madam,*
      In accordance with your request we have sent you under separate cover our
      pattern book of armchair covers for your selection.
      We look forward to receiving your order which *will have* our *immediate*
      attention.
      Yours faithfully,
      For and on behalf of
      GLORIOUS FURNISHING MATERIALS LIMITED

5.   **D Ms Brijs,**
      Wtufyordv 10 Jun nd wrpltcnfm tht wwlbabl t dzpch th tw grmnts uhv
      chozn wthn th nxfwdys.
      Azrng u ovrbstn atltms.
      Ysn,
      Jaqln Nwcm
      Suprvzr Cstmr Srvzs

5a.   *Dear* Miss Bridges,
      We thank you for your order of the 10 June and *we are pleased to confirm*
      that *we will be able* to despatch the two garments you have chosen within
      the next few days.
      Assuring you *of our best attention at all times.*
      Yours sincerely,
      Jaqueline Newcombe
      Supervisor Customer Services

6.   **Ftnv - Mr Jon Wyz**
      Wlyms & Wyz
      Slztrs
      Hgh St
      Wrthg
      Susx

      Dsr,
      Mrs. Hnryta Hwpr
      Bunglw - 5 Dhlsd Grdns, Th Grov, Wrthg, Suzx
      Fbhfv mi abvnmd clynt Impltehfytn th tytl Dds rlhtg t th abvmn
      proprty.
      Y urjatn t thsmtr wdb aprzytd.
      Yf,

6a. For attention of - Mr John Wise
Williams & Wise
Solicitors
High Street
Worthing
Sussex

Dear Sir,
Mrs Henrietta Hooper
Bungalow - 5 Daleside Gardens, The Grove, Worthing, Sussex
For and on behalf of my *above named* client *I am pleased to enclose herewith for your attention* the Title Deeds relating to the *above mentioned* property.
Your *urgent attention* to *this matter* would be appreciated.
Yours faithfully,

7. **Fabrzi Fyn Lthr Fshns**
Rom
Wakrvytlx. Pltusno asnsucn th xpctd dt v arvl v y rprsntv n Lndn so tht wcn rsrv th nzsry htl acmdzn.
Bsrgds
Drctr
Vog Lthr Aczsrys Ltd

7a. Fabrizzi Fine Leather Fashions
Rome
We acknowledge receipt of your telex. Please let us know as soon as you can the expected date of arrival of your representative in London so that we can reserve the necessary hotel accommodation.
Best regards,
Director
Vogue Leather Accessories Ltd

8. **Swft Nzrnz Brokrs**
Dsrs,
Mrs. Brbra Colns
Wrfr t th trvl nzrnz tkn ot onbhfv th abvnmd cvrng hr rsnt tw wks hldy on th Frnch Rvyra nd wreh clm fm gvg fulprtcs v hr clm f rmbrzmnt f dmj t hr lugj cntng clthg nd prsnl efcts wylst it ws n trnzt.
Wawt ztlm v th clm ndwcs.
Yf,
Arwnd & Abwt Trvl Ajnts

8a. Swift Insurance Brokers:
Dear Sirs,
Mrs. Barbara Collins
We refer to the travel insurance taken out *on behalf of* the *above named* covering her recent two weeks holiday on the French Riviera and *we are enclosing herewith* claim form giving *full particulars* of her claim for reimbursement for damage to her luggage containing clothing and personal effects, whilst it was in transit.
We await settlement of the claim *in due course.*
Yours faithfully,
Around & About Travel Agents

9. **T: Nhznwyd Bwk Splyrs**
Dsrs,
Frthtmytlcn v tdysdt nfmg u tht Ihv stl nt rzvd th prsl v bwks snt t m ovr tw wks ago. Nthsrcms, pls b gd enf t chk wnz agn wth th pstl awthrtys, or crdt m wth th cst nvolvd.
Yurjatn t thsmtr wdb aprzytd.
Yf,
S. Chrchl

9a. To: Nationwide Book Suppliers
Dear Sirs,
Further to my telephone conversation of *today's date* informing you that *I have* still not received the parcel of books sent to me over two weeks ago. *In the circumstances,* please be good enough to check once again with the postal authorities, or credit me with the cost involved.
Your urgent attention to *this matter would be* appreciated.
Yours faithfully,
S. Churchill

10. **D Mr Brly,**
Cnupls fwrd t m th acwnt dtls rqnmylv 5 Fbwry. Nvwv th urjnzy v thsmtr, Iwd aprzyt th dtls rqrd brp.
Tnkg u n antzpzn v y imdatn t myrq.
Yf,
Malcm Carlyl

10a. *Dear* Mr Burleigh,
Can you please forward to me the account details *requested in my letter of* 5th February. *In view of* the urgency of *this matter, I would* appreciate the details required *by return post.*
Thanking you in anticipation of your *immediate attention* to *my request.*
Yours sincerely,
Malcolm Carlisle

11. Dsr,

    Wtufynqv ydysdt nd wrpltnfmu tht wcn imdytly sply th sx foldg chrs u rqr. Pltusno whn itwlbcnv t dlvr thz gds ty prems. Wlkfwrd t hrng frmu atyerlcnv nd azrng u ovrbstn atltms.

    Yf,

    R. Jonsn

    Zls Cordnhtr

    Zls Dpt

11a. Dear Sir,

    We thank you for your enquiry of yesterday's date and we are pleased to inform you that we can immediately supply the six folding chairs you require. Please let us know when it will be convenient to deliver these goods to your premises. We look forward to hearing from you at your earliest convenience and assuring you of our best attention at all times.

    Yours faithfully,

    R. Johnson

    Sales Co-ordinator

    Sales Department

12. D Mr Tompsn

    Frthtur tdystlcn, wrgrt t lrn tht th elctrc blnkt rsntly purchzd frm ur stor hz prvd tb fwlty. Pls rtrn it tus asnsucn nd wwl rfund th pstj cst. Nthmntm, w r sndg u a rplazm dbl sz blnkt.

    Pls acpt ur snzr apljys f nyncnv czd tu nthsmtr.

    Ysn,

    Chrls Patrsn

    Cmplnts Dpt

12a. Dear Mr Thompson,

    Further to our today's telephone conversation, we regret to learn that the electric blanket recently purchased from our store has proved to be faulty. Please return it to us as soon as you can and we will refund the postage cost. In the meantime, we are sending you a replacement double size blanket. Please accept our sincere apologies for any inconvenience caused to you in this matter.

    Yours sincerely,

    Charles Patterson

    Complaints Department

CHAPTER 19

BUILDING BLOCKS

The following examples illustrate how the **ROOT WORD** is **built-up** by the addition of **prefixes and/or suffixes, terminations, or additional syllables.**

Prefixes: - 'com=cm' 'con=cn' 'dis=ds' 'en=n' 'recom=rcm'
          - 'per=pr' 'sub=sb'
Suffixes: - 'ing=g' 'sion=zn' 'tion=zn'
          - 'ment=m' following a consonant

mend	mnd
amend	amnd
amending	amndg
commend	cmnd
commending	cmndg
recommend	rcmnd
recommending	rcmndg

main	mhn
remain	rmhn
remaining	rmhng
remainder	rmhndr

commit	**cmt**
committing	**cmtg**
omit	**omt**
omitting	**omtg**
remit	**rmt**
remitting	**rmtg**
permit	**prmt**
permitting	**prmtg**
submit	**sbmt**
submitting	**sbmtg**

cashing	**cshg**
encashing	**ncshg** ('en = n')
encash	**ncsh**
encashing	**ncshg**
encashment	**ncshm**

commence	**cmnz**
commencing	**cmnzg**
commencement	**cmnzm**
commensurate	**cmnzrht**
re**commence**	**rcmnz**
re**commencing**	**rcmnzg**
re**commencement**	**rcmnzm**

Prefixes: - 'dis = ds', 'rea = ry'
Suffix: - 'ing = g', 'ring = rng'

mission	**mzn**
com**mission**	**cmzn**
per**mission**	**prmzn**
re**mission**	**rmzn**
sub**mission**	**sbmzn**
missionary	**mznry**

count	**cwnt**
counting	**cwntg**
counter	**cwntr**
dis**count**	**dscwnt**
dis**counting**	**dscwntg**
en**counter**	**ncwntr**
en**countering**	**ncwntrng**

appear	**apr**
appearing	**aprng**
appearance	**aprnz**
dis**appear**	**dsapr**
dis**appearing**	**dsaprng**
dis**appearance**	**dsaprnz**
re**appear**	**rypr**
re**appearing**	**ryprng**
re**appearance**	**ryprnz**

real	**ryl**
realise	**ryl**z
realising	**ryl**zg
realisation	**ryl**zn
mate**rial**	mt**ryl**
mate**rial**ise	mt**ryl**z
mate**rial**ising	mt**ryl**zg
mate**rial**isation	mt**ryl**zn

side	**sd**
in**side**	n**sd**
out**side**	ot**sd**
de**cide**	d**sd**
re**side**	r**sd**

Prefixes: 'com = cm', 'con = cn'
'de = d', 'ex = x'
'im = m', 'in = n', 'sub = sb'

position	**pzn**
cm**position**	cm**pzn**
de**position**	d**pzn**
im**position**	m**pzn**
pro**position**	pro**pzn**
su**position**	s**pzn**

compose	**cmpz**
depose	**dpz**
expose	**xpz**
impose	**mpz**
propose	**propz**
suppose	**spz**

com	**cm**
be**come**	b**cm**
be**com**ing	b**cm**g
in**come**	n**cm**
in**com**ing	n**cm**g

assist	**asst**
assisting	**asst**g
consist	c**nsst**
consisting	c**nsst**g
desist	d**sst**
desisting	d**sst**g
insist	n**sst**
insisting	n**sst**g
persist	pr**sst**
persisting	pr**sst**g
resist	r**sst**
resisting	r**sst**g
subsist	sb**sst**
subsisting	sb**sst**g

exist	xst
existing	xstg
existence	xstnz

assistance	asstnz
consistent	cnsstnt
insistence	nsstnz
persistence	prsstnz
resistance	rsstnz
subsistence	sbsstnz

(Dipthong 'rea = ry')

rise	rz
arising	arzg
arisen	arzn
rearise	ryrz
rearising	ryrzg
rearisen	ryrzn
prize	prz
aprise	aprz
aprising	aprzg
aprisal	aprzl
reprise	rprz
reprising	rprzg
reprisal	rprzl
surprise	srprz
surprised	srprzd
surprising	srprzg

co-exist	coxst
co-existing	coxstg
co-existence	coxstnz

Prefixes: 'con = cn',
'in = 'n'

form	fm('Short')
forming	fmg
formation	fmzn
conform	cnfm
conforming	cnfmg
conformation	cnfmzn
inform	nfm
informing	nfmg
information	nfmzn

claim	clm
acclaim	aclm
acclaiming	aclmg
acclamation	aclmzn
exclaim	xclm
exclaiming	xclmg
exclamation	xclmzn
disclaim	dsclm
disclaimer	dsclmr
proclaim	proclm
proclamation	proclmzn

Prefixes: - 'con = cn', 'in = n', 'per = pr', 'sub = sb'
Suffixes: - 'ing = g', 'sion/tion = zn'

avert	avrt
averting	avrtg
convert	cnvrt
converting	cnvrtg
divert	dvrt
diverting	dvrtg
invert	nvrt
inverting	nvrtg
revert	rvrt
reverting	rvrtg
version	vrzn
aversion	avrzn
diversion	dvrzn
inversion	nvrzn
reversion	rvrzn
subversion	sbvrzn

part	prt
party	prty
parting	prtg
partnership	prtnrshp
compartment	cmprtmt
depart	dprt
department	dprtm*
impart	mprt
imparting	mprtg
impartment	mprtm
(* can be 'dpt')	

('wing = wng')
(Dipthong 'ua = w')

value	vlw
valuing	vlwng
valuation	vlwzn
evalue	evlw
evaluating	evlwtg
evaluation	evlwzn
devalue	dvlw
devaluing	dvlwng
devaluation	dvlwzn
revalue	rvlw
revaluing	rvlwng
revaluation	rvlwzn
valuable	vlwbl
invaluable	nvlwbl

merge	mrj
merger	mrjr
merging	mrjg
emerge	emrj
emerging	emrjg
emergence	emrjnz
submerge	sbmrj
submerging	sbmrjg

Suffix: 'sion' following 'press' = 'sn'

press	**prs**
pressing	**prs**g
com**press**	cm**prs**
com**press**ing	cm**prs**g
com**press**ion	cm**prs**n
de**press**	d**prs**
de**press**ing	d**prs**g
de**press**ion	d**prs**n
ex**press**	x**prs**
ex**press**ing	x**prs**g
ex**press**ion	x**prs**n
im**press**	m**prs**
im**press**ing	m**prs**g
im**press**ion	m**prs**n
re**press**	r**prs**
re**press**ing	r**prs**g
re**press**ion	r**prs**n
sup**press**	s**prs**
sup**press**ing	s**prs**g
sup**press**ion	s**prs**n

(zure/sure = zr)
(rise/risation = rz/rzn)

p**ressure**	**przr**
pres**sur**ise	**przrz**
pres**sur**ising	**przrzg**
pres**sur**isation	**przrzn**

(Dipthong: 'rea' = 'ry')
Prefix: 'recon' = rcn'

firm	**fhm**
af**firm**	a**fhm**
af**firm**ing	a**fhm**g
af**firm**ation	a**fhm**zn
con**firm**	cn**fhm**
con**firm**ing	cn**fhm**g
con**firm**ation	cn**fhm**zn
re**affirm**	ry**fhm**(rea = ry)
re**affirm**ing	ry**fhm**g
re**affirm**ation	ry**fhm**zn
recon**firm**	rcn**fhm**
recon**firm**ing	rcn**fhm**g
recon**firm**ation	rcn**fhm**zn

Prefixes: 'en' = 'n', 'rein = rn')

force	**fz** ('Short')
forcing	**fz**g
en**forc**e	n**fz**
en**forc**ing	n**fz**g
en**forc**ement	n**fz**m
rein**forc**e	rn**fz**
rein**forc**ing	rn**fz**g
rein**forc**ement	rn**fz**m

(Termination 'cise/size' = 'sz')

p**recise**	**prsz**
p**recise**ly	**prsz**ly
p**recis**ion	**prsz**n

additional form:-

con**firm**	**cnfrm**
con**firm**ing	**cnfrmg**
con**firm**ation	**cnfrmzn**

AgiliWriting

*Refer to end of book.

EXERCISES

GROUPS A - Y

Read and copy the 'Agiliwriting' shorthand sentences:
'Strings' are *italicised*. 'Shorts' are underlined

GROUP A

1) *Can you* please send us on approval *as soon as you can* an assortment <u>of</u> <u>your</u> attractive accessories as advertised.

1a) *Cnu* pls snd us on aprvl *asnsucn* an asortm v y atrctv aczsrys as advrtzd.

2) We <u>are</u> aware <u>that</u> <u>the</u> announcement appertaining <u>to</u> <u>the</u> amalgamation *will not be* acceptable <u>to</u> all the members <u>of</u> our association.

2a) W r awr tht th anwnzm aprtng t th amlgmzn *wlntb* acptbl t al th mmbrs v ur asozn.

3) *In reply to your enquiry of yesterday's date, we have* ascertained <u>from</u> <u>the</u> agents <u>that</u> the office accommodation *as well as* all its amenities *will be* <u>made</u> available <u>to</u> a company <u>of</u> architects in August.

3a) *Nrptynqv ydysdt, whv* asrtnd frm th ajnts tht th ofz acmdzn *aswls* al its amntys *wlb* md avlbl t a cmpny v arctcts n Awgst.

4) Although the actuarial assessment is arguable, *we have* asked the assessors to augment the amount of your claim as quickly as possible and they are now awaiting their accountants approval.

4a) **Altho th actwryl azsmnt s argwbl, *whv* askd th azsrs t awgm th amwnt v y clm as qkly as psbl nd thy r nw awtg thyr acwntnts aprvl.**

5) We are appending for your authorisation a list of the alternative annual appointments soon *to be* advertised. We are afraid that there *will be* only an average amount of applicants actually applying *in view of* the awkward activities anticipated.

5a) **W r apndg f y awthrzn a lst v th altrnhtv anwl apntms sn *tb* advrtzd. W r afrhd tht thr *wlb* only an avrj amwnt v aplcnts actwly aplyg *nvwv* th awkwrd actvtys antzptd.**

6) We agree to accept your offer of actual assistance and we appreciate the amount *to be* advanced *to us* as it will alleviate our anxieties.

6a) **W agr t acpt y ofr v actwl asstnz nd w aprzyt th amwnt *tb* advnzd *tus* as it wl alvyt ur anxytys.**

7) Are we to assume that their audacious assumptions *will be* applauded and approved as an accurate assessment of the atrocious affair?

7a) **R w t azm tht thyr awdshz azmpns *wlb* aplwdd nd aprvd as an acrht azsmnt v th atroshz afhr?**

8) We appreciate the adequate advice given *to us* about the assembly of the amazing apparatus *as well as* the additional assistance afforded *to us*.

8a) **W aprzyt th adqt advs gvn *tus* abwt th azmbly v th amzg aprhtz *aswls* th adznl asstnz afdd *tus*.**

9) We are altogether adamant about his admittance to the Association as we agree *with you* that he has admirable administrative abilities which *could be* very advantageous to all of us.

9a) **W r altgthr admnt abwt hs admtnz t th Asozn as w agr *wthu* tht h hz admrbl admnstrhtv abltys wch *cdb* vry advntjyz t al v us.**

10)   I wish to advise you that I appreciate your astute advice and *I am* acutely aware of all the advantages which may accrue to me. *As soon as* I have ascertained the actual amenities available, *I* will accordingly take the appropriate action.

10a)   **I wsh t advz u tht I aprzyt y astwt advs nd *Im* acwtly awr v al th advntjys wch my acrw t m.** *Asns* **I hv asrtnd th actwl amntys avlbl,** *Iwl* **acdgly tk th apropryt acn.**

11)   They appear *to be* accumulating *a lot of* archaeological antiquities at the auction *as well as* additional ancient articles.

11a)   **Thy apr** *tb* **acmlhtg** *alotv* **arcyljcl antqtys at th awcn** *aswls* **adznl anznt artcls.**

'Shorts' (words in this category contain consonants only.)
Read and copy:-
1.   and/**nd**, answer/**nsr**
2.   any/**ny**, anyway/**nywy**, anywhere/**nywhr**, anyone/**nywn**

GROUP B
Read and copy the 'Agiliwriting' shorthand sentences:

1)   *We wish* to advise you that your borrowing at the bank has been very heavy this year. We believe *it would* benefit you if *we were* to *give you* a breakdown of your balances.

1a)   *Wwsh* **t advz u tht y borwng at th bnk hzbn vry hvy ths yr. W blv it wd bnft u if** *wwr* **t** *gvu* **a brkdwn v y blnzs.**

2)   *We were* hoping to obtain a better bargain at the bigger sales but the best ones had been bought by the time we arrived.

2a)   *Wwr* **hpg to obtn a btr brgn at th bgr zls bt th bst wns hd bn bawt bi th tym w arvd.**

3)   Business has *not been* very busy due to the fact that *we* have *not yet* brought out our brochure.

3a)   **Bznz** *hzntbn* **vry bzy dw t th fct tht** *whvnt* **yt brawt ot ur broshr.**

4)   We believe <u>that</u> our bookings <u>for</u> <u>holidays</u> abroad <u>are</u> behind due <u>to</u> the <u>break</u> in the weather.

4a)   **W blv tht ur bwkgs f hldys abrwd r bhnd dw t th brk n th wethr.**

5)   *I will be* booking the best <u>possible</u> *bed and breakfast* accommodation *on behalf of* my brother before he arrives here from Belgium in May.

5a)   *Iwlb* **bwkg th bst psbl** *bdnbrkfst* **acmdzn** *onbhfv* **mi brothr bfr h arvs hre frm Bljm n My.**

6)   *We have* benefitted by taking a bridging loan from the bank and *we will be* budgeting for this when we buy the building.

6a)   *Whv* **bnftd bi tkg a brijg lwn frm th bnk nd** *wwlb* **bujtg f ths whn w by th bldg.**

'Shorts' (words in this category contain consonants only)
Read and copy:-
1.   bank/**bnk**, banking/**bnkg**, banker/**bnkr**
2.   base/**bz**, basing/**bzg**, basic/**bzc**, basically/**bzcly**
3.   being/**bng**, become/**bcm**, becoming/**bcmg**, beside/**bsd**, behalf/**bhf**, behind/**bhnd**, before/**bfr**, beforehand/**bfrhnd**, belong/**blng**, belonging/**blngng**, beyond/**bynd**
4.   bill/**bl**, billing/**blg**, built/**bld**, builder/**bldr**,
5.   busy/**bzy**, busier/**bzyr**, busiest/**bzyst**
      buy/**by** (**by** = **bi**), buyer/**byr**, buying/**byg**

GROUP C
Read and copy the 'Agiliwriting' shorthand sentences:

1)   *In the circumstances* we agree to accept cancellation of <u>your</u> <u>cheque</u> <u>for</u> the cannisters as *you have* always been a courteous <u>and</u> considerate <u>customer.</u>

1a)   *Nthsrcms* **w agr t acpt cnslhzn v y chq f th cnstrs as** *uhv* **alwys bn a crtyz nd cnsdrht cstmr.**

2)　　We <u>are</u> certain <u>you</u> will <u>find</u> the cabin conditions <u>very</u> comfortable <u>and</u> we <u>are</u> confident <u>that</u> no other <u>company</u> is currently offering a comparable cheap cruise to the Carribean.

2a)　**W r srtn tht uwl fnd th cabn cndzns vry cmftbl nd w r cnfdnt tht no othr cmpny s crntly ofrng a cmprhbl chp crwz t th Crhbyn.**

3)　　We confirm <u>that</u> *we* <u>*can*</u> offer a <u>low</u> <u>cost</u> comprehensive service to all our <u>customers</u> as it <u>is</u> <u>of</u> great concern <u>to</u> <u>us</u> <u>that</u> every <u>care</u> <u>is</u> <u>taken</u> <u>to</u> <u>cover</u> all contingencies so <u>that</u> <u>there</u> *will* *be* no cause for complaint.

3a)　**W cnfhm tht w cn ofr a lw cst cmprhnzv srvz t al ur cstmrs as it s v grht cnsrn *tus* tht evry cr s tkn t cvr al cntnjnzys so tht thr *wlb* no cz f cmplnt.**

4)　　We feel *it* *would* *be* advisable <u>for</u> the corporation <u>to</u> conserve its <u>capital</u> <u>because</u> <u>of</u> the continuing currency complications <u>in</u> the <u>country.</u>

4a)　**W fl *itwdb* advzbl f th crprhzn t cnsrv its cptl bcz v th cntnwng crnzy cmplczns n th cntry.**

5)　　*We* *have* acquainted our customers <u>with</u> <u>your</u> catalogue <u>of</u> creative casual clothes <u>and</u> co-ordinates *as* *well* *as* <u>your</u> other conventional costumes in acrylic cloths <u>and</u> <u>they</u> <u>will</u> be <u>calling</u> <u>to</u> see <u>your</u> considerable collection as *soon* *as* *they* *can.*

5a)　**Whv aqntd ur cstmrs wth y ctlog v crytv czwl clwths nd cordnhts *aswls* y othr cnvnznl cstwms n acrlc cloths nd thy wlb clg t z y cnsdrbl clcn *asnsthycn.***

6)　　We <u>hope</u> *you* *can* attend our annual celebrations. Please <u>check</u> <u>your</u> other committments and confirm by correspondence whether *you* *will* *be* coming. *We* *look* *forward* to your co-operation *in* *this* *matter*.

6a)　**W hp *ucn* atnd ur anwl slbrhzns. Pls chk y othr cmtmnts nd cnfhm bi crspndnz whthr *uwlb* cmg. Wlkfwd t y coprhzn *nthsmtr.***

7)   Our commercial commitments <u>are</u> a considerable charge on <u>our</u> company's capital and *we can* only consider <u>contracts</u> capable <u>of</u> an early conclusion.

7a)   **Ur cmrzl cmtmnts r a cnsdrbl chrj on ur cmpnys cptl nd *wcn* only cnsdr cntrcts cpbl v an erly cnclzn.**

8)   *We acknowledge receipt of* your circular containing a list <u>of</u> <u>your</u> <u>goods</u> for export. *Can you please* confirm that <u>your</u> prices are competitive in the commercial climate <u>of</u> our <u>country.</u>

8a)   ***Wakrv* y srclr cntng a lst v y gds f xpt. *Cnupls* cnfhm tht y prcs r cmptv n th cmrzl clymt v ur cntry.**

9)   *It will not be* very convenient for our Chairman to attend the meeting on the day advised *by you* <u>because</u> <u>of</u> the congestion in the city centre at that *time of day.*

9a)   ***Itwlntb* vry cnvnynt f ur Chrmn t atnd th mtg on th dy advzd bu bcz v th cnjstn n th zty sntr at tht *tmvdy.***

10)   We regret <u>to</u> learn <u>that</u> *you have* <u>cause</u> <u>to</u> complain about the <u>case</u> you bought <u>from</u> us. We <u>cannot</u> agree <u>that</u> it is cumbersome <u>and</u> <u>not</u> worth the <u>cost.</u> *Can you please let us* <u>have</u> it <u>back</u> <u>and</u> if we believe <u>your</u> <u>claim</u> is correct we <u>are</u> prepared to <u>change</u> it <u>for</u> another, or credit you with a <u>cheque</u> or <u>cash.</u>

10a)   **W rgrt t lrn tht u hv cz t cmpln abwt th cs u bawt frm us. W *cnt* agr tht it s cmbrsm nd nt wrth th cst. *Cnupls ltus* hv it bk nd if y clm s crct w r prprd t chnj it f anthr, or crdt u wth a chq or csh.**

11)   <u>Any</u> corporation entering into a <u>contract</u> <u>with</u> a <u>customer</u> must exercise the utmost <u>caution.</u> Terms and conditions *should be* clearly stated. The <u>method</u> <u>of</u> calculation of commission *should be* concisely <u>set</u> out and confirmation obtained <u>of</u> <u>any</u> commercial <u>customs</u> <u>to</u> <u>take</u> into consideration.

11a)   **Ny crprhzn ntrng nto a cntrct wth a cstmr mz xrsz th utmoz czn. Trms nd cndzns *shdb* clrly statd. Th mthd v clclhzn v cmzn shdb cnszly zt ot nd cnfhmzn obtnd v ny cmrzl cstms t tk nto cnsdrhzn.**

12) The competition <u>for</u> the charter <u>contract</u> <u>was</u> very keen <u>and</u> *we have had* to consider insurance cover, compensation <u>claims</u>, consignment classifications, <u>and</u> other complicated clauses, before coming to a decision.

12a) **Th cmptzn f th chrtr cntrct wz vry kn nd *whvhd* t cnsdr nzrnz cvr, cmpnzsn clms, nd othr cmplctd clwzs bfr cmg t a dszn.**

13) The *cash and carry* company deals in cheap cotton <u>goods</u> and other commodities.

13a) **Th cs*hnc*ry cmpny dls n chp cotn gds nd othr cmodtys.**

14a) The Conservative candidate is certain to gain a considerable <u>majority</u> following his colossal campaign.

14a) **Th cnsrvtv cnddt s srtn t ghn a cnsdrbl mjrty folwng hs clozl cmpn.**

15) The <u>company</u> <u>has</u> a large clientele <u>because</u> <u>of</u> the comprehensive services it <u>can</u> offer clients countrywide.

15a) **Th cmpny hz a lrj clyntl bcz v th cmprhnzv srvzs it cn ofr clynts cntrywyd.**

16. A *lot of* new business *has been* created through our contacts in Czechoslovakia.

16a) **A lotv nu bznz hzbn crytd thru ur cntcts n Chkslovka.**

'SHORTS' (words in this category contain consonants only.)
Read and copy:-

1. cash/**csh,** cashier/**cshr**, chair/**chr**, chairman/**chrmn**,
   Chairmanship/**chrmnshp**
2. charge/**chrj**, charging/**chrjg**
3. call/**cl**, caller/**clr**, calling/**clg**, clear/**clr**, clearer/**clrhr**, clearing/**clrng**
4. change/**chnj**, changing/**chanjg**, chance/**chnz**, chancing/**chnzg**, chancellor/**chnzlr**

5.   can/**cn**, cannot/**cnt**, copy/**cpy**, copied/**cpyd**, copier/**cpyr**
6.   cheque/chq, check/chk
7.   correspond/**crspnd**, corresponding/**crspndg**, correspondence/**crspndnz**
8.   cost/**cst**, costed/**cstd**, costing/**cstg**
9.   credit/**crdt**, crediting/**crdtg**, creditor/**crdtr**
10.   cover/**cvr**, covered/**cvrd**, covering/**cvrng**
11.   custom/**cstm**, customer/**cstmr**
12.   current/**crnt**, currently/**crntly**, currency/crnzy
13.   correct/**crct**, correcting/**crctg**, correction/**crcn**
14.   contract/**cntrct**, contracted/**cntrctd**, contractor/**cntrctr**
15.   claim/**clm**, claiming/**clmg**, claimant/**clmnt**

GROUP D

Read and copy the 'Agiliwriting' shorthand sentences:

1)   The delegates <u>have</u> decided against attending the conference due <u>to</u> the differences <u>of</u> opinion within the delegation about the matters to be discussed.

1a)   **Th dlgts hv dsdd agnst atndg th cnfrnz dw t th dfrnzs v opnyn wthn th dlgzn abwt th matrs *tb* dscuzd.**

2)   We <u>are</u> determined <u>to</u> dissuade the distinguished company <u>from</u> deferring their visit <u>to</u> this department. <u>To</u> delay *would not be* desirable <u>and</u> the consequences <u>would</u> be detrimental <u>and</u> disadvantageous <u>to</u> all concerned.

2a)   **W r dtrmnd to dswad th dstngwshd cmpny frm dfrng thyr vzt t ths dptm. T dlhy *wdntb* dzrbl nd th cnsqnzs *wdb* dtrmntl nd dsadvntjyz t al cnsrnd.**

3)   Please <u>give</u> us full details <u>of</u> <u>the</u> deficits in deliveries <u>and</u> when <u>they</u> <u>can</u> be <u>despatched.</u> We <u>are</u> <u>very</u> <u>much</u> disturbed by these discrepancies.

3a)   **Pls gv us ful dtls v th dfzts n dlvrys nd whn thy *cnb* dzpchd. W r vry mch dstrbd bi thz dscrpnzys.**

4)   The developers <u>were</u> deluged by determined conservationists who were desperate <u>to</u> avoid the damaging consequences of development <u>and</u> the disastrous destruction <u>of</u> the delightful countryside.

4a)   Th dvlprs wr dlwjd bi dtrmnd cnsrvznsts who wr dzprht t avwd th dmjg cnsqnzs v dvlpmnt nd th dsztrwz dstrucn v th dlytfl cntrysd.

5)   We definitely disagree with the deductions shown in <u>your</u> invoice. We <u>are</u> <u>very</u> disappointed as *we were* depending upon you to give us an additional discount.

5a)   W dfntly dsagry wth th dducns shwn n y nvz. W r vry dsapntd as *wwr* dpndg upn u t gv us an adznl dscwnt.

6)   The development <u>of</u> decentralisation <u>has</u> drawn different departments <u>to</u> destinations distant from the central office <u>and</u> a certain duplication in the controlling of divisions *can be* distinguished.

6a)   Th dvlpmnt v dsntrlzn hz drwn dfrnt dptmnts t dstnhzns dstnt frm th sntrl ofz nd a srtn dwplczn n th cntrlg v dvzns cnb dstngwshd.

7)   The effect <u>of</u> disinvestment *has been* detrimental <u>and</u> disappointing <u>and</u> it is doubtful whether dividends <u>will</u> <u>double</u> this year.

7a)   Th efcts v dsnvstm *hzbn* dtrmntl nd dsapntg nd it s dwtfl whthr dvdnds wl dbl ths yr.

8)   *It will be* <u>very</u> difficult <u>to</u> deliver the deposits, documentation, <u>and</u> drafts <u>to</u> the director <u>today,</u> <u>but</u> we <u>are</u> determined <u>not to</u> <u>let</u> the distance deter us.

8a)   *Itwlb* vry dfclt t dlvr th dpzts, dcmntzn nd drfts t th drctr tdy, bt w r dtrmnd nt t lt th dstnz dtr us.

9)   *We will* derive no benefit <u>from</u> the deteriorating conditions in the division. It is apparent <u>that</u> diversification <u>has</u> <u>caused</u> <u>some</u> disruption and we <u>are</u> determined <u>not to</u> depend upon them or the dealers when <u>they</u> arrive <u>from</u> Denmark.

9a)   *Wwl* drv no bnft frm th dtryrhtg cndzns n th dvzn. It s aprnt tht dvrzfczn hz czd sm dsrupn nd w r dtrmnd nt t dpnd upn thm or th dlrs whn thy arv frm Dnmrk.

10)   One <u>must</u> insist on the devotion <u>to</u> discipline in the training <u>of</u> delinquents <u>to</u> avoid the danger <u>of</u> disintegration <u>of</u> our society.

10a) **Wn mz nsst on the dvozn t dspln n th trhng v dlnqnts t avwd th dnjr v dsntgrhzn v ur sozty.**

'SHORTS' (words in this category contain consonants only.)
Read and copy:-

1.   day/**dy**, daily/**dly**, deliver/**dlvr**, delivery/**dlvry**/dlivering/**dlvrng**
2.   dear/**d**, doctor/**dr**
3.   dental/**dntl**, dentist/**dntst**, detail/**dtl**, detailing/**dtlg**
4.   depart/**dprt**, departing/**dprtg**
5.   done/**dn**, does/**dz**, did/**dd**, did not/**ddnt**, down/**dwn**, doing/**dwng**
6.   develop/**dvlp**, developer/**dvlpr**, developing/**dvlpg**
7.   difficult/**dfclt**, difficulty/**dfclty**
8.   despatch/**dzpch**, despatching/**dzpchg**, despatchment/**dzpchm**
9.   dispatch/**dspch**, dispatching/**dspchg**, dispatchment/**dspchm**
10.   discharge/**dschrj**, discharging/**dschrjg**, distant/**dstnt**, distance/**dstnz**
11.   discover/**dscvr**, discovery/**dscvry**
12.   document/**dcmnt**, documenting/**dcmntg**, doumentation/**dcmntzn**
13.   direct/**drct**, director/**drctr**, directing/**drctg**, directive/**drctv**
14.   draft/**drft**, drafting/**drftg**

GROUP E

Read and copy the 'Agiliwriting' shorthand sentences:

1)   *We have* engaged an excellent engineer <u>to</u> examine the environmental conditions <u>and</u> after an exhaustive examination it <u>has</u> emerged <u>that</u> <u>there</u> <u>are</u> essential electrical works to be executed.

1a)   **Whv ngjd an xlnt njnr t xmn th nvrnmntl cndzns nd aftr an xwstv xmnhzn it hz emrjd tht thr r esnzl elctrcl wrks tb xcwtd.**

2)   *Please let us have* evidence <u>of</u> the excessive expenditure <u>that</u> you embarked upon after the emergency <u>was</u> enforced.

2a)   **Pltushv evdnz v th xzsv xpndtur tht u mbrkd upn aftr th emrjnzy wz nfzd.**

3) We encourage <u>and</u> expect all employees, before <u>they</u> <u>are</u> engaged, <u>to</u> extensively examine their terms <u>of</u> employment <u>to</u> ensure <u>that</u> the terms <u>and</u> conditions <u>are</u> equivalent <u>with</u> their expectations.

3a) **W ncrj nd xpct al mployes bfr thy r ngjd t xtnsvly xmn thyr trms v mploym vry crfuly t nzr tht th trms nd cndzns r eqvlnt wth thyr xpctzns.**

4) It is essential <u>to</u> extend the existing educational establishments before the expiration <u>of</u> another year. The extensions envisaged will enable all entrants to enjoy their full educational entitlement.

4a) **It s esnzl t xtnd th xstg edwcznl estblshms bfr th xprhzn v anthr yr. Th xtnzns nvzjd wl nabl al ntrnts t njy thyr ful edwcznl ntytlm.**

5) We expect *to be able* <u>to</u> eventually eliminate the embarrassing conditions experienced by everyone at the Embassy, <u>but</u> *it will not be* easy to extradite the extravagant elements.

5a) **W xpct *tbabl* t evntwly elmnht th mbrhzg cndzns xprynzd bi evrywn at th Mbzy, bt *itwlntb* ezy t xtrdyt th xtrvgnt elmnts.**

6) We <u>cannot</u> entertain the extras embodied in the estimate as <u>they will</u> create expenses <u>which</u> <u>are</u> extreme <u>and</u> even extortionate. *We have* ensured <u>that</u> the excessive <u>costs</u> <u>will</u> <u>not</u> escalate <u>still</u> further as it is essential <u>to</u> economise.

6a) **W cnt ntrtn th xtras mbdyd n th estmt as thy will cryt xpnzs wch r xtrm nd evn xtorznht. *Whv* enzrd tht th xzsv csts wl nt esclht stl frthr as it s esnzl t ecnomz.**

7) *We must be* enabled *as far as possible* <u>to</u> <u>have</u> examples <u>of</u> the efficiency <u>and</u> expertise <u>of</u> each <u>of</u> the engineers before <u>they</u> embark upon the examination <u>of</u> the exceptionally complicated electronic systems.

7a) ***Wmzb* nabld *asfrspsb* t hv xmpls v th efznzy nd xprtz v ech v th njnrs bfr thy mbrk upn th xmnhzn v th xzpnly cmplctd elctronc sstms.**

8)   Even though the expenses <u>for</u> doing up the establishment were extraordinarily high, <u>there</u> <u>are</u> extenuating circumstances as the works executed <u>were</u> of an exellent standard.

8a)   **Evn tho th xpnzs f dwng up th estblshm wr xtrwrdnrly hgh, thr r xtnwtg srcmstnzs* as th wrks xcwtd wr v an xlnt stndrd.**
*Can be **'srcms'**

9)   We <u>are</u> exerting all our efforts into erecting the exciting art exhibition, <u>but</u> we will endeavour <u>to</u> eventually enlist <u>some</u> extra help from the experts.

9a)   **W r xrtg al ur efrts nto erctg th xytg art xbzn bt wwl ndvr t evntwly nlst sm xtra hlp frm th xprts.**

10)   *We can* only enthuse and <u>say</u> without exaggeration <u>that</u> the evenings entertainment <u>was</u> enjoyed by everyone.

10a)   **Wcn only nthwz nd sy wthot xajrhzn tht th evngs ntrtnm wz njyd bi evrywn.**

'SHORTS' (words in this category contain consonants only.)
Read and copy:-

1.   enforce/**nfz**, enforcing/**nfzg**, enforcement/**nfzm**
2.   encourage/**ncrj**, encouraging/**ncrjg**, encouragement/**ncrjm**

GROUP F
Read and copy:

1.   Following upon the favourable facts forwarded *tus,* we <u>will</u> facilitate the financing <u>of</u> the fertilizer factory so <u>that</u> contracts *can be* finalised.

1a)   **Folwng upn th fvrbl fcts fwrdd** *tus,* ***wwl* fzltt th fnanzg v th frtlzr fctry so tht cntrcts** *cnb* **fnlzd.**

2)   *We will not* fail <u>to</u> fix the faulty fire fighting equipment *as soon as we can.*

2a)   **Wwlnt fhl t fx th fwlty fyr fytg eqpm** *asnswcn.*

3)   Please request the Federation to familiarise themselves <u>with</u> the forms and after filling them in, *they should be* return *to us* without fail within the next fortnight.

3a)   **Pls rqst th Fdrhzn t fmlyrz thmslvs wth th fms nd aftr filg thm n *thysdhb* rtrnd *tus* wthot fhl wthn th nxt ftnyt.**

4)   The freehold house includes fashionable furniture, fixtures and fittings, <u>but</u> we feel *it will not* fetch the formidable figure envisaged.

4a)   **Th frhld hwz nclwds fshnbl frntur, fxturs nd fitgs, bt w fl it wl nt fch th fmdbl fgr nvzjd.**

5)   Please <u>give</u> us *as far as you can* an account <u>of</u> the fluctuating figures in the foreign markets *as well as* in other faraway fields.

5a)   **Pls gv us *asfrsucn* an acwnt v th fluctwtg fgrs n th frn mrkts *aswls* n othr frhwy flds.**

6)   We <u>are</u> in favour <u>of</u> fitting further fluorescent lights and other first class fitments in the offices on the first floor.

6a)   **W r n fvr v fitg frthr flrsnt lyts nd othr frst clz ftmnts n th ofzs on th frst flr.**

7)   *We have been* forced to forfeit the contract forwarded *to us in view of* the fact that we are unable to fulfil their far fetched formulas.

7a)   **W *hvbn* fzd t forft th cntrct fwrdd *tus nvwv* th fct tht *wrunbl* t fulfl thyr far fchd fmlas.**

8)   It is fortunate <u>that</u> <u>your</u> friends <u>have</u> found it better to forgive <u>and</u> forget in a matter which <u>has</u> foolishly *been* fought over <u>for</u> so long.

8a)   **It s ftwnht tht y frnds hv fwnd it btr t fgv nd fgt n a matr wch hz fwlshly bn fawt ovr f so lng.**

9)   The friendly fellows <u>are</u> <u>from</u> a flourishing family firm dealing in fine foods <u>and</u> flavourings.

9a)   **Th frndly felws r frm a flrshg fmly fhm dlg n fyn fwds nd flvrngs.**

10)   It <u>is</u> our feeling foreigners *should not* fail <u>to</u> forearm themselves against <u>any</u> unfavourable forecast as it <u>is</u> impossible <u>to</u> foresee <u>what</u> <u>they</u> will face financially <u>in</u> the future.

10a) **It s ur flg frnrs shdnt fhl t forarm thmslvs agnst ny unfvrbl fcast as its mpsbl t f'z wht thy wl fs fnanzly n th futr.**

11)   It <u>is</u> frustrating <u>that</u> the facts forwarded *to us* appear *to be* without foundation <u>and</u> even fictitious.

11a) **It s frustrhtg tht th fcts fwrdd *tus* apr tb wthot fwndzn nd evn fctshz.**

12)   <u>There</u> is no doubt <u>that</u> the fire in the field <u>was</u> caused by the flammable conditions. The flare <u>from</u> the fire *could be* seen <u>from</u> far-off.

12a) **Thr s no dwt tht th fyr n th fld wz czd bi th flambl cndzns. Th flar frm th fyr cdb zn frm farov.**

13)   Please *do not* forget to forward *to us* the facts concerning the forthcoming fair.

13a) **Pls *dnt* fgt t fwrd tus th fcts cnsrng th fthcmg fhr.**

14)   The bright foliage <u>of</u> the flowers created quite a flamboyant display.

14a) **Th bryt folyj v th flowrs crytd qte a flmbwnt dsply.**

15)   The flight to France *has been* booked for next Friday. I *must not* forget to buy some French Francs.

15a) **Th flyt t Frnz *hzbn* bwkd f nxt Frdy. I *mznt* fgt t by sm Frnch Frncs.**

'SHORTS' (words in this category contain consonants only).
Read and copy:

1.   find/**fnd**, finding/**fndg**
2.   fact/**fct**, factory/**fctry**
3.   fashion/**fshn**, fashionable/**fshnbl**
4.   favour/**fvr**, favouring/**fvrng**, favourable/**fvrbl**
5.   forward/**fwrd**, forwarding/**fwrdg**, forwarder/**fwrdr**
6.   figure/**fgr**, figuring/**fgrng**
7.   final/**fnl**, finality/**fnlty**
8.   forthcoming/**fthcmg**, further/**frthr**, freehold/**frhld**

GROUP G
Read and copy the 'Agiliwriting' shorthand sentences:

1)   *We were* grateful <u>for</u> the guarantee given to us <u>that</u> the green garden gates *would be* delivered before the weekend.

1a)   *Wwr* grtfl f th grnty gvn tus tht th grn grdn ghts *wdb* dlvrd bfr th wknd.

2)   *We have* gained great satisfaction <u>from</u> the <u>fact</u> <u>that</u> the Government is giving generous grants to new businesses.

2a)   Whv ghnd grht stsfcn frm th fct tht th Gvmnt s gvg jnrwz grnts t nu bznzs.

3)   The <u>directors</u> were greeted <u>with</u> congratulations on their announcement <u>that</u> the gross profits <u>of</u> the gardening equipment group <u>had</u> <u>gone</u> up greatly this year.

3a)   Th drctrs wr grtd wth cngrtlhzns on thyr anwnzm tht th groz profts v th grdng eqpm grwp hd gn up grtly thsyr.

4)   The garments advertised in the gazette <u>are</u> gaining ground *as far as* fashion goes. It is generally agreed <u>that</u> the generous cut is very fashionable *at the present time.*

4a)   **Th grmnts advrtzd n th gazt r ghng grwnd *asfrs* fshn gwz. Its jnrly agrd tht th jnrwz cut s vry fshnbl *athprsntm*.**

5)   We <u>are</u> grieved by the fact <u>that</u> the general conditions and lack <u>of</u> generosity shown to the group *did not* generate any goodwill.

5a)   **W r grvd bi th fct tht th jnrl cndzns nd lak v jnrozty shwn t th grwp *ddnt* jnrht ny gwdwl.**

6)   The genial German gentleman <u>was</u> a genius at geography.

6a)   **Th jnyl Jrmn jntlmn ws a jnyz at jygrfy.**

7)   We generally get our geraniums <u>and</u> other <u>goods</u> <u>from</u> the gardening centre.

7a)   **W jnrly gt ur jrhnyms nd othr gds frm th grdng sntr.**

8)   *It would be* a generalisation to say that they <u>are</u> always generous.

8a)   **It would be** a jnrlzn t sy tht thy r alwys jnrwz.

9)   Our Greek guest *could not* grapple with the guessing game.

9a)   **Ur Grk gst *cdnt* grapl wth th gzg gm.**

10)   The girls were grateful to their gentle guardian for her guidance.

10a) **Th grls wr grtfl t thyr jntl grdyn f hr gydnz.**

11)   It is <u>taken</u> <u>for</u> <u>granted</u> <u>that</u> a gratuity is <u>given</u> <u>to</u> <u>show</u> gratitude <u>for</u> <u>good</u> service.

11)   **It s tkn f grntd tht a gratwty s gvn t shw gratwd f gd srvz.**

12)   Guidelines on <u>good</u> food were <u>given</u> <u>to</u> me by a gourmet <u>with</u> a gigantic appetite.

12a) **Gydlyns on gd fwd wr gvn t m bi a gwrmy wth a jygntc aptyt.**

'SHORTS' (words in this category contain consonants only).
Read and copy:

1.   get/**gt**, gone/**gn**, give/**gv**, giving/**gvg**
2.   grateful/**grtfl**, garment/**grmnt**, guarantee/**grnty**
3.   Government/**Gvmnt**, garden/**grdn**, gardener/**grdnr**, gardening/**grdng**, game/**gm**

GROUP H

Read and copy the 'Agiliwriting' shorthand sentences:

1)   We hesitate <u>to</u> handle household hardware as our last experience in this field <u>was</u> horrible.

1a)   **W hztt t hndl hwzhld hrdwr as ur lzt xprynz n ths fld wz horbl.**

2)   *We have been* asked by Headquarters to obtain an honest assessment of the horrendous housing conditions.

2a)   ***Whvbn* askd bi Hdqrtrs t obtn an hnst azsmnt v th horndwz hwzg cndzns.**

3)   *I was not* happy to hear* from her* husband <u>that</u> she <u>has</u> been ill ever since her* arrival here* <u>from</u> Hanover. I <u>have</u> assured him however, <u>that</u> *I would be* <u>happy</u> <u>to</u> <u>give</u> her a helping <u>hand</u> with the housework.

3a)   **I *wznt* hpy t hr* frm hr husbnd tht sh *hzbn* il evr snz hr arvl hr* frm Hnovr. I hv azrd hm hwvr, tht *Iwdb* hpy t gv hr a hlpg hnd wth th hwzwrk.**
*Agilityping: 'hear = hrh', 'here = hre'.

4)   We are afraid <u>that</u> the <u>cost</u> <u>for</u> haulage *will be* higher <u>than</u> *we can* <u>happily</u> afford.

4a)   **W r afrhd tht th cst f hwlj wlb hghr thn *wcn* hply afd.**

5)   *We have* heard that big hampers *have been* hired by the <u>hotel</u> near here.

5a)   ***Whv* hrd tht bg hamprs *hvbn* hyrd bi th htl nr hre.**

6)   *I am* <u>very</u> dissatisfied with the haphazard heating in this house *as it does not* function at all well.

6a)   **Im vry dstsfd wth th hphzrd htg n ths hwz as it dznt funcn at al wel.**

7)   We hear* that he is buying a new house near here* and we wish him every happiness in his new home.

7a)   **W hrh* tht h s byg a nu hwz nr hre* nd w wsh hm evry hpynz n hs nu hom.**

*Agilityping

8)   *We were* handicapped by habitual harassement during our journey to the harbour <u>to</u> see the handmade handicrafts. It <u>made</u> the going <u>very</u> heavy.

8a)   **Wwr hndycapd bi hbtwl hrazmnt drng ur jrny t th hrbr t z th hndmd hndycrfts. It md th gwng vry hvy.**

'SHORTS' (words in this category contain consonants only).
Read and copy:

1.   he/**h**, her/**hr**, herself/**hrslf**, himself/**hmslf**, him/**hm**, his/**hs**
2.   health/**hlth**, healthy/**hlthy**
3.   hand/**hnd,** handkerchief/**hndkrchf,** happen/**hpn**, happening/**hpng**, happened/**hpnd**
4.   hope/**hp**, hopeful/**hpfl**, hopefully/**hpfuly**
5.   hardly/**hrdly**, hardship/**hrdshp**
6.   has/**hs**, had/**hd**, have/**hv**, having/**hvg**
7.   hang/**hng**, hanging/**hngng**
8.   help/**hlp**, helped/**hlpd**, helping/**hlpg**
9.   hereby/**hrby**, herein/**hrn**, hereunder/**hrundr**
10.   holiday/**hldy**, hospital/**hsptl**, hotel/**htl**, hotelier/**htlyr**

GROUP I

Read and copy the 'Agiliwriting' sentences.

1) *We have been* informed <u>that</u> there *will be* intensive industrialisation in this sector and *in the circumstances* we <u>are</u> <u>hoping</u> <u>to</u> increase our <u>sales</u>.

1a) ***Whvbn* nfmd tht thr *wlb* ntnzv ndstrylzn n ths sctr nd nthsrcms w r hpg t ncrz ur zls.**

2) *We were* <u>very</u> interested in the independent <u>and</u> innovative ideas <u>of</u> the influential Indian gentleman we interviewed. *We have* intimated that we intend inviting him to speak on other issues.

2a) **Wwr vry ntrstd n th ndpndnt nd inovtv idys v th nflwnzl Ndyn jntlmn w ntrvwd. Whv ntmtd tht w ntnd nvtg hm t spk on othr izws.**

3) The Inspector initiated an intensive investigation after the incident and it seemed to him that the irregularities were due to the inexperience <u>of</u> the people involved.

3a) **Th Nspctr nshytd an ntnzv nvstgzn aftr th nzdnt nd it zmd t hm tht th irglrtys wr dw t th nxprynz v th ppl nvolvd.**

4) We <u>are</u> indeed <u>sorry</u> <u>that</u> *we cannot* intervene in the Institute's ruling in this instance as it *would be* improper <u>of</u> us <u>to</u> interfere.

4a) **W r ndd sry tht w cnt ntrvn n th Nstwt's rwlg n ths nstnz as itwdb mpropr v us t ntrfr.**

5) It is important <u>that</u> the insertion in <u>your</u> next issue will induce interest in the items indicated.

5a) **It s mptnt tht th nsrzn n y nxt izw wl ndwz ntrst n th itms ndctd.**

6) *It will be* imperative <u>to</u> isolate the infants <u>from</u> the infection. The inferior conditions inside the infirmary are inexcusable.

6a) **Itwlb mprhtv t izlht th nfnts frm th nfcn. Th nfryr cndzns nsd th nfhmry r nxcwzbl.**

7)   *I am* impressed by the incredible increase in value of the freehold investment in the immediate vicinity.

7a)   *Im* mprsd bi th ncrdbl ncrz n vlw v th frhld nvstm n th imdyt vznty.

8)   I intend interceding *on behalf of* the innocent Innkeeper as it is my innate feeling that the irrational incident of incitement was brought about by the irrate interloper.

8a)   **I ntnd ntrzdg onbhfv th inosnt Nkpr as it s mi inht flg tht th iraznl nsdnt v nzytm wz brawt abwt bi th irht ntrlopr.**

9)   The improvements in exports invite international expansion and investment and *we have been* inundated with requests for information about incentives and other important issues.

9a)   **Th mprvmnts n xpts nvt ntrnznl xpanzn nd nvstmnt nd *whvbn* nundtd wth rqsts f nfmzn abwt nsntvs nd othr mptnt izws.**

10)   We regret our inability to inspect the imported goods without the intervention of independent assessors and we look to your insurers to indemnify us against loss of income and any other expenses which *may be* incurred.

10a)   **W rgrt ur nablty t nspct th mptd gds wthot th ntrvnzn v ndpndnt azsrs nd w lwk t y nzrhrs t ndmnfy us agnst loz v ncm nd ny othr xpnzs wch myb ncrd.**

11)   We are indeed sorry about the indiscretions which occurred *as well as* the impetuous, irritating and intimidating behaviour of the instigators.

11a)   **W r ndd sry abwt th ndscrzns wch ocrd *aswls* th mptwz, iryttg nd ntmdtg bhvyr v th nstgtrs.**

12)   It is inadvisable that the payment of instalments *should be* so irregular and we are inclined to institute immediate proceedings for recovery of the balance outstanding unless *you can* assure us that there *will be* an impressive improvement.

12a) It s nadvzbl tht th pmnt v nstalmnts shdb so irglr nd w r nclnd t nstwt imdyt prozdgs f rcvry v th blnz otstndg unls ucn azr us tht thr wlb an mprsv mprvm.

13) The insurance company <u>have</u> <u>made</u> an inspection <u>and</u> they insist <u>that</u> unless the insecure doors <u>in</u> the <u>factory</u> <u>are</u> immediately seen <u>to</u> they <u>cannot</u> implement the insurance.

13a) Th nzrnz cmpny hv md an nspcn nd thy nsst tht unls th nscwr drs n th fctry r imdytly zn t thy cnt mplmnt th nzrnz.

14) The instructions <u>for</u> the operation <u>of</u> our Ideal instruments appear on pages 6 to 9 <u>of</u> the illustrated leaflet. <u>Kindly</u> indicate <u>your</u> intentions by initialling on the index each item <u>in</u> <u>which</u> <u>you</u> <u>are</u> interested. We will invoice you for any increases or incidentals.

14a) Th nstrucns f th oprhzn v ur Idyl nstrmnts apr on pjs 6 t 9 v th ilstrhtd lflt. Kndly ndct y ntnzns bi nshlg on th ndx ech itm n wch u r ntrstd. Wwl nvz u f ny ncrzs or nzdntls.

15) It is imperative that the Italians are introduced to the influential industrial group. Your initiative in this instance would inject an impressive ingredient insofaras invoking ideal internal intercommunication. They insist that our inability in this instance could incite irreconcilable internal differences.

15a) It s mprhtv tht th Itlyns r ntrdwzd t th nflwnzl ndstryl grwp. Y nshtv n ths nstnz wd njct an mprsv ngrdynt nsofars nvokg idyl ntrnl ntrcmnczn. Thy nsst tht ur nablty n ths nstnz cd nzyt ircnzlbl ntrnl dfrnzs.

16) Our Chairman is indecisive about accepting <u>your</u> invitation as it <u>will</u> inconvenience <u>him</u> *in view of* his other important commitments, *as well as* being an imposition which will interfere with impending international interviews.

16a) Ur Chrmn s ndszv abwt acptg y nvtzn as it wl ncnvnynz* hm *nvwv* hs othr mptnt cmtms, *aswls* bng an mpzn wch wl ntrfr wth mpndg ntrnznl ntrvws.

*Can be 'ncnv'

'SHORTS' (words in this category contain consonants only.)
Read and copy:

1.   in/**n**, is/**s**
2.   impossible/**mpsbl**, impossibility/**mpsblty**
3.   import/**mpt**, important/**mptnt**, importance/**mptnz**

GROUP J

Read and copy the 'Agiliwriting' shorthand sentences:

1)   The joint venture enjoyed great success.

1a)   **Th jnt vntur njyd grht sczs.**

2)   Our journal <u>for</u> the younger generation <u>has</u> <u>just</u> been <u>published.</u>

2a)   **Ur jrnl f th yngr jnrhzn hz jst bn pblshd.**

3)   We <u>are</u> awaiting the outcome <u>of</u> the judicial enquiry.

3a)   **W r awtg th otcm v th jwdzl nqry.**

4)   The gorgeous jewels were imported <u>from</u> Japan.

4a)   **Th gorjyz jwls wr mptd frm Jpn.**

5)   The judgement <u>may</u> <u>not</u> <u>have</u> a <u>very</u> jovial outcome.

5a)   **Th jujm my nt hv a vry jovyl otcm.**

6)   There *could be* no justification <u>in joining</u> <u>forces</u> <u>with</u> <u>them</u> at this juncture.

6a)   **Thr *cdb* no jstfczn n jng fzs wth thm at ths junctr.**

'SHORTS' (words in this category contain consonants only.)
Read and copy:

1.   just/**jst**, justified/**jstfd**, justifying/**jstfyg**, justification/**jstfczn**
2.   journey/**jrny**, journal/**jrnl**, journalist/**jrnlst**, journalism/**jrnlsm**
3.   join/**jn**, joining/**jng**, joint/**jnt**, jointly/**jntly**

GROUP K
Read and copy the 'Agiliwriting' shorthand sentences:

1) *We have* asked them if *they would be* <u>kind</u> enough to keep the Kindergarten open a few hours longer *this week.*

1a) *Whv* askd thm if thy *wdb* knd enuf t kp th Kndrgrtn opn a fw hwrs lngr *thswk.*

2) *Thank you* very <u>much</u> for the king size kettle you lent me.

2a) *Tnku* vry mch f th kng sz ketl u lnt m.

3) Kindly return the keys <u>you</u> <u>have</u> kept.

3a) Kndly rtrn th kys u hv kpt.

4) The keeper <u>of</u> the keys *can be* found <u>in</u> the kitchen.

4a) Th kpr v th kys cnb fwnd n th kchn.

5) The keyboards *can be* safely operated by anyone keying in information of any kind.

5a) Th kybrds cnb sfly oprhtd bi nywn kyg n nfo v ny knd.

6) The cook <u>was</u> <u>busy</u> <u>in</u> the kitchen cooking Kedgeree, Chicken Kiev <u>and</u> braised kidneys.

6a) Th cwk wz bzy n th kchn cwkg Kjry, Chkn Kyv nd brhzd kdnys.

7) The cook <u>was</u> keen <u>to</u> know <u>where</u> the long knives were kept.

7a) Th cwk wz kn t kno whr th lng nyvs wr kpt.

8) The child kept on kissing <u>and</u> cuddling the sweet <u>little</u> kitten.

8a) Th chld kpt on ksg nd cudlg th swt ltl ktn.

'SHORTS' (words in this category contain consonants only).
Read and copy:

1.   kind/**knd,** kindly/**kndly,** kindness/**kndnz**

GROUP L
Read and copy the 'Agiliwriting' shorthand sentences:

1)   *We regret to inform you* <u>that</u> the <u>company</u> <u>has</u> <u>gone</u> into   liquidation as
       it no <u>longer</u> <u>has</u> a licence to <u>trade</u>.

1a)   *Wrgrtnfmu* **tht th cmpny hz gn nto lqdzn as it no lngr hz a lznz t trd.**

2)   The letter <u>lets</u> us know <u>that</u> there is <u>likely</u> *to be* a <u>lower</u> limit on the level
       of lending allowed. *We will be* <u>left</u> <u>with</u> <u>little</u> leeway.

2a)   **Th ltr lts us kno tht thr s lkly tb a lwr lmt on th lvl v lndg alwd. Wwlb
       lft wth ltl lwy.**

3)   *Please let us know* the location <u>of</u> the property. There seems to be less and
       less to look at these days.

3a)   *Pltusno* **th lczn v th lzhld proprty. Thr zms tb** *lsnls* **t lwk at thz dys.**

4)   The <u>local</u> authority <u>is</u> losing <u>labour</u> <u>to</u> other Boroughs. There is a lesson
       to be learned from this, however laborious <u>that</u> *may be*.

4a)   **Th lcl awthrty s lwzg lbr t othr Boros. Thr s a lson** *tb* **lrnd frm
       ths, hwvr lbryz tht** *myb.*

5)   The leading party *has been* steadily losing ground. It looks like their
       outlook is <u>not</u> liberal enough.

5a)   **Th ldg prty** *hzbn* **stedly lwzg grnd. It lwks lk thyr otlwk s nt lbrl enuf.**

6)   *We will not be* liable <u>for</u> the luggage left <u>in</u> the locker after the last day <u>of</u>
       the month.

6a)   *Wwlntb* **lybl f th lugj lft n th lokr aftr th lzt dy v th mnth.**

7)   The location *has been* a <u>longstanding</u> <u>local</u> attraction.

7a)   **Th lczn *hzbn* a lngstndg lcl atrcn.**

8)   *You will be* liable <u>for</u> <u>any</u> loss arising <u>from</u> the litigation <u>to do</u> <u>with</u> the case <u>of</u> libel.

8a)   ***Uwlb* lybl f ny loz arzg frm th ltgzn tdo wth th cs v libl.**

9)   *We do not* <u>like</u> the <u>low</u> lighting <u>in</u> the large room. A little spotlight <u>would</u> enlarge the lighting capacity.

9a)   ***Wdnt* lk th lw lytg n th lrj rm. A ltl spotlyt wd nlrj th lytg cpzty.**

10)   We <u>are</u> <u>not</u> impressed by the terms <u>of</u> the loan as <u>set</u> out <u>in</u> the letter sent *to us* by the lenders as we appear *to be* losing out <u>in</u> the *longterm*.

10a)   **W r nt mprsd bi th trms v th lwn as zt ot n th ltr snt *tus* bi th lndrs as w apr tb lwzg ot n th *lngtrm*.**

11)   It is <u>likely</u> <u>that</u> the livlihoods of those in the <u>business</u> <u>of</u> lending *will be* less lucrative due to the limitations on lending and other legalities imposed by the legislation.

11a)   **It s lkly tht th lyvlhwds v thoz n th bznz v lndg *wlb* ls lwcrhtv dw t th lmtzns on lndg nd othr lgltys mpzd bi th ljslhzn.**

12)   We loved the luxurious lounge <u>in</u> the leasehold property, *as well as* its locality. We were loath to leave it.

12a)   **W lovd th luxryz lwnj n th lzhld proprty, *aswls* its lczn. W wr loth t lv it.**

13)   *I was* nearly late for the luncheon laid on by the literary group <u>to</u> promote their literature. The loquacious leading writer had a lot to say about logistics.

13a)   ***I wz* nrly lht f th lunchn lhd on bi th ltrhry grwp t promt thyr ltrhtr. Th loqshz ldg wrtr hd a lot t sy abwt lojstcs.**

14) Our last lodger drove locomotives.

14a) **Ur lzt lojr drov lcmotvs.**

'SHORTS' (words in this category contain consonants only).
Read and copy:

1. listen/**lzn**, listener/**lznr**, listening/**lzng**
2. last/**lzt**, lasting/**lztg**, lasted/**lztd**
3. large/**lrj**, largely/**lrjly**.
4. like/**lk**, liken/**lkn**, likely/**lkly**.
5. low/**lw**, lower/**lwr**, lowering/**lwrng**, lowered/**lwrd**

GROUP M
Read and copy the 'Agiliwriting' shorthand sentences:

1) The manufacturing margins are low and we must mark up the goods to make a profit.

1a) **Th mnfctrng mrjns r lw nd w mz mrk up th gds t mk a proft.**

2) *We have* your message regarding the materials and we must apologise for the misunderstanding due to misrepresentation of the facts.

2a) **Whv y mzj rgrdg th mtryls nd w mz apljz f th msundrstndg dw t msrprsntzn v th fcts.**

3) Following our move the mail was misdirected and we missed the meeting.

3a) **Folwng ur mv th mhl wz msdrctd nd w msd th mtg.**

4) We expect to deliver the machines in the middle of the month.

4a) **W xpct t dlvr th mshns n th mdl v th mnth.**

5)   The modernisation of the factory and the incorporation of many marvellous modifications has greatly minimised maintenance.

5a)   **Th modrnzn v th fctry nd th ncrprhzn v mny mrvlwz modfczns hz grhtly mnmzd mhntnz.**

6)   As mentioned in your memorandum, *it would be* a mistake to engage someone to undertake the management of the main department. I might send a memo about this to the Managing Director.

6a)   **As mnznd n y mmrndm *itwdb* a mstk t ngj smwn t undrtk th mnjm v th mhn dprtm. I myt snd a mmo abwt ths t th Mnjg Drctr.**

7)   We must say *we have* some misgivings about the market and it might be better to delay the manufacture of the material until after midsummer.

7a)   **W mz sy w hv sm msgvgs abwt th mrkt nd it myt b btr t dlhy th mnfctr v th mtryl untl aftr mdsumr.**

8)   The membership has managed to maintain its marvellous monthly magazine.

8a)   **Th mmbrshp hz mnjd t mhntn its mrvlwz mnthly mgzn.**

9)   *We will* meet in the middle of the month to discuss mainly the matter of the mysterious misdirection of the medical supplies and other miscellaneous merchandise.

9a)   ***Wwl* mt n th mdl v th mnth t dscuz mhnly th matr v th mstryz msdrcn v th mdcl splys nd othr mslnyz mrchndz.**

10)   The millionaire has bought a magnificent mansion by the mediterranean.

10a)   **Th mlynhr hz bawt a mgnfznt manzn bi th mdtrhnyn.**

11)   The Minister's memoirs about the militant maneouvres within the administration might be regarded by the Ministry as mischievous

11a)   **Th Mnstr's mmwrs abwt th mltnt mnwvrs wthn th admnstrhzn myt b rgdd bi th Mnstry as mschvwz.**

'SHORTS' (words in this category contain consonants only).
Read and copy:

1.   month/**mnth**, monthly/**mnthly**
2.   make/**mk**, making/**mkg**, made/**md**
3.   manufacture/**mnfctr**, manufacturing/**mnfctrng**, manufacturer/**mnfctr**
4.   margin/**mrjn**, marginal/**mrjnl**
5.   mark/**mrk**, market/**mrkt**, marketing/**mrktg**
6.   must/**mz**, move/**mv**, moving/**mvg**
7.   mistake/**mstk**, mistakem/**mstkn**

GROUP N
Read and copy the 'Agiliwriting' shorthand sentences:

1)   *Please let us have* your *name, address and telephone number* so that *you can be* notified *if need be.*

1a)   **Pls** *ltushv* **y** *nmadrzntlno.* **so tht** *ucnb* **ntfd if ndh b.**

2)   Nevertheless, it is necessary to note your nationality in your application as this is now needed. The formalities nowadays are a nightmare.

2a)   **Nvrthls, it s nzsry t nte y naznlty n y aplczn as ths s nw ndhd. Th fmltys nwadys r a nytmhr.**

3)   *We have* never said that the newspaper *will not* appear *next month.*

3a)   **Whv nvr zd tht th nwspapr** *wlnt* **apr nxmnth.**

4)   Nothing more *has been* noted about negotiations. The non-alliance in this respect is not normal.

4a)   **Nthg mor hzbn ntd abwt ngozns. Th nnalynz n ths rspct s nt nrml.**

5)   It is a nuisance the way nationalisation of the industry has become so negative.

5a)   **It s a nwsnz th wy naznlzn v th ndstry hz bcm so ngtv.**

6)   Our Nationwide network means <u>that</u> we neglect <u>none</u> of our customers.

6a)   **Ur Nhznwyd ntwrk mns tht w nglct nn v ur cstmrs.**

7)   *Please let us have* news <u>of</u> <u>your</u> next week's campaign on nutritious natural foods.

7a)   *Plsltushv* **nws v y nxt wk's cmpn on nwtrshz natrl fwds.**

8)   *Would you* please give notification <u>to</u> the committee to be neither negligent nor nervous about the <u>number</u> <u>of</u> new nominations <u>for</u> the national post.

8a)   *Wdu* **pls gv ntfczn t th cmty** *tb* **nthr ngljnt nor nrvwz abwt th nmbr v nu nomnhzns f th nznl pst.**

9)   My neighbours feel neutral about the neglected areas <u>of</u> land nearby. Its a nuisance <u>that</u> their views are so non-committal.

9a)   **Mi nhbrs flh nwtrl abwt th nglctd arys v land nrby. Its a nwznz tht thyr vws r so nncmtl.**

10)   I prefer a neighbourhood <u>that</u> is nice and quiet. Needless to say, noisy neighbours <u>are</u> <u>not</u> desirable at any time.

10a) **I prfr a nhbrhwd tht s nyz nd qyt. Ndls t sy, nzy nhbrs r nt dzrbl at ny tym.**

'SHORTS' (words in this category contain consonants only).
Read and copy:

1. name/**nm**, named/**nmd**, namely/**nmly**
2. number/**nmbr**, numbering/**nmbrng**
3. now/**nw**, nothing/**nthg**, not/**nt**

GROUP O

1)   We <u>are</u> pleased <u>to</u> say we obtained the order <u>for</u> the ornaments we offered <u>to</u> supply <u>to</u> the overseas organisation. *It will be* an ongoing opportunity if *we can* overcome the original overheads.

1a)   **W r plsd t sy w obtnd th ordr f th ornmnts w ofrd t sply t th ovrzs orgnzn. *Itwlb* an ongwng oprtnty if *wcn* ovrcm th orjnl ovrhds.**

2)   These obligations occur occasionally <u>from</u> our ownership <u>of</u> the goods.

2a)   **Thz oblgzns ocr ocznly frm ur ownrshp v th gds.**

3)   The bank official advised us to observe the <u>fact</u> <u>that</u> we <u>are</u> overdrawn.

3a)   **Th bnk ofzl advzd us t obsrv th fct tht w r ovrdrwn.**

4)   We <u>are</u> <u>of</u> the opinion <u>that</u> the opposition occurred over the fact <u>that</u> the objectionable occupants are <u>not</u> the real owners <u>of</u> the outbuilding.

4a)   **W r v th opnyn tht th opzn ocrd ovr th fct tht th objcnbl ocpnts r nt th ryl ownrs v th otbldg.**

5)   We <u>are</u> sure <u>that</u> the bank *have been* overcharging us on   <u>our</u> overdraft.

5a)   **W r zr tht th bnk *hvbn* ovrchrjg us on ur ovrdrft.**

6)   The outcome <u>of</u> the overseas operation <u>has</u> shown <u>that</u> it <u>was</u> well organised.

6a)   **Th otcm v th ovrzs oprhzn hz shwn tht it wz wel orgnzd.**

7)   It is obvious <u>that</u> the organisation <u>have</u> kept the offices in <u>good</u> order since their occupation.

7a)   **It s obvyz tht th orgnzn hv kpt th ofzs n gd ordr snz thyr ocpzn.**

8)   *We must not* overlook the overheads and the overtime rates payable to our operatives, otherwise, they will become overwhelming.

8a)   ***Wmznt* ovrlwk th ovrhds nd th ovrtym rhts pybl t ur oprhtvs, othrwz, thy wl bcm ovrwelmg.**

9) The item is outstanding <u>because</u> it <u>was</u> omitted <u>from</u> the order <u>but</u> no-one noticed it.

9a) **Th itm s otstndg bcz it wz omtd frm th ordr bt nown ntzd it.**

10) The owners <u>are</u> ordinarily <u>very</u> obedient about observing the official rules relating <u>to</u> the parking <u>of</u> vehicles outside the offices.

10a) **Th ownrs r ordnrly vry obdynt abwt obsrvg th ofzl rwls rlhtg t th parkg v vhcls otsd th ofzs.**

'SHORTS' (words in this category contain consonants only).
Read and copy:

1. our/**ur**, ourselves/**urslvs**
2. out/**ot**, outcome/**otcm**
3. ought/**owt**

GROUP P
Read and copy the 'Agiliwriting' shorthand sentences:

1. The popularity <u>of</u> the party is increasing *all the time*.

1a. **Th poplrty v th prty s ncrzg** *althtm.*

2) *We will* try to persuade him to <u>take</u> up the proposition as we believe *it will be* <u>very</u> profitable *to do* so.

2a) ***Ww/** **try t prswad hm t tk up th propzn as w blv** *itwlb* **vry proftbl** *tdoso.*

3) <u>Your</u> proposals as shown in the <u>marketing</u> projection <u>are</u> phenomenal. *We will* certainly pursue them.

3a) **Y propzls as shwn n th mrktg projcn r fnomnl.** *Ww/* **srtnly przw thm.**

4) <u>For</u> psychological reasons we propose <u>to</u> prevent the publication <u>of</u> the photographs.

4a) **F sycljcl rsns w propz t prvnt th pblczn v th ftogrfs.**

5) Preparation <u>of</u> the printed publications *will be* completed after provision <u>of</u> the proofs.

5a) **Prprhzn v th prntd pblczns *wlb* cmpltd aftr provzn v th prwfs.**

6) We <u>are</u> packing the pieces <u>of</u> material preferred by the purchaser.

6a) **W r pkg th pcs v mtryl prfrd bi th prchzr.**

7) The prosperous proprietor thinks that it is <u>of</u> paramount importance <u>to</u> persever <u>in</u> the promotion <u>of</u> business.

7a) **Th prosprwz proprytr thnks tht it s v prhmwnt mptnz t prsvr n th promzn v bznz.**

8) *It will be* our practice <u>to</u> increase our production as much *as we can.* We must persist in persuading our personnel to be punctual in the performance of their particular posts.

8a) **_Itwlb_ ur practz t ncrz ur producn as much *aswcn*. W mz prsst n prswadg ur prsnel *tb* punctwl n th prfmnz v thyr prtclr psts.**

9) The proposal concerning the promissory note *will not be* acceptable <u>to</u> us.

9a) **Th propzl cnsrng th promsry nte *wlntb* acptbl t us.**

10) *We have* previously applied precautionary measures <u>to</u> prevent payment <u>of</u> large premiums.

10a) ***Whv* prvyzly aplyd prycznry mzrs t prvnt pmnt v lrj prmyms.**

ll) We perceived <u>that</u> the <u>police</u> were present at the political party speech <u>day</u> <u>to</u> retain the peace.

11a) **W przvd tht th plz wr prsnt at th poltcl prty spch dy t rtn th pz.**

12) The political problems pertaining <u>to</u> the partition <u>are</u> unlikely *to be* publicised. We know a <u>number</u> <u>of</u> petitions <u>have</u> already been <u>passed.</u>

12a) **Th poltcl problms prtng t th prtzn r unlkly tb pblszd. W kno a nmbr v ptzns hv alrdy bn psd.**

13) The painter painting the paintwork <u>in</u> the palatial <u>rooms</u> <u>of</u> the palace is <u>making</u> excellent progress.

13a) **Th pntr pntg th pntwrk n th plhzl rms v th plhz s mkg xlnt progrz.**

14) I propose <u>to</u> peruse the publications <u>when</u> <u>they</u> <u>are</u> printed; particularly the paragraphs pertaining <u>to</u> pensions.

14a) **I propz t prwz th pblczns whn thy r prntd; prtclrly th prhgrfs prtng t pnzns.**

15) The political party organised a parade <u>to</u> popularise themselves <u>with</u> the people.

15a) **Th poltcl prty orgnzd a prhd t poplrz thmslvs wth th ppl.**

16) The pianist gave a perfect performance in the pavilion.

16a) **Th pynst gav a prfct prfmnz n th pvlyn.**

17) The professoris considered *to be* a perfectionist <u>in</u> his profession.

17a) **Th profzr s cnsdrd *tb* a prfcnst n hs profzn.**

18) We <u>are</u> particularly perturbed by the procrastination <u>of</u> the President <u>in</u> implementing the policies.

18a) **W r prtclrly prtrbd bi th procrstnhzn v th Prsdnt n mplmntg th polzys.**

19) It is perhaps possible <u>that</u> one's position <u>could</u> remain pecuniary by being "penny wise <u>and</u> pound foolish".

19a) **It s prhps psbl tht wn's pzn cd rmhn pcwnry bi bng "pny wyz nd pwnd fwlsh".**

20) *Please let us know* the precise prices <u>of</u> the paperback publications being produced. We <u>are</u> being pressed by the public <u>to</u> provide the one on 'Public Parks'.

20a) *Plsltusno* **th prsz prcs v th paprbk pblczns bng prodzd. W r bng prsd bi th pblc t provd th wn on "Pblc Parks".**

21) Despite the pressure put upon us, we <u>are</u> <u>not</u> prepared <u>to</u> participate <u>in</u> the public demonstration planned to <u>take</u> place as we prefer <u>to</u> maintain the peace.

21a) **Dspyt th przr put upn us, w r nt prprd t prtzpt n th ppblc dmnstrhzn pland t tk plaz as w prfr t mhntn th pz.**

22) The poet personally presented a book of his poetry to the photographer.

22a) **Th pwt prsnly prsntd a bwk v hs pwtry t th ftogrfr.**

'SHORTS' (words in this category contain consonants only).
Read and copy:

1.   pay/**py**, paid/**pd**, paying/**pyg**, payer/**pyr**
2.   pack/**pk**, packed/**pkd**, packing/**pkg**, packer/**pkr**
3.   paint/**pnt**, painter/**pntr**, painting/**pntg**
4.   part/**prt**, parting/**prtg**, partner/**prtnr**
5.   pleasure/**plzr**, pleasant/**plznt**, pleasurable/**plzrbl**
6.   purchase/**prchz**, purchsing/**prchzg**, purchaser/**prchzr**
7.   post/**pst**, postpone/**pstpn**, postponement/**pstpnmnt**
8.   print/**prnt**, printer/**prntr**, printing/**prntg**

GROUP Q
Read and copy the 'Agiliwriting' shorthand sentences.

1)   We <u>are</u> querying the quantities <u>shown</u> in <u>your</u> quotation <u>for</u> this quarter.

1a)   **W r qryg th qntys shwn n y qwtn f ths qrtr.**

2)   We asked the fellow <u>to</u> quit *in view of* his questionable qualifications.

2a)   **W askd th felw t qt *nvwv* hs qstnbl qlfczns.**

3)   There were queues <u>of</u> people outside the palace hoping <u>to</u> see the Queen.

3a)   **Thr wr qws v ppl otsd th plhz hpg t z th Qn.**

4)   There were quite a lot of questions which <u>had</u> *to be* quickly answered in the quiz.

4a)   **Thr wr qte a lot v qstns wch hd *tb* qkly ansrd n th qz.**

5)   Our main quest is <u>to</u> quit the noisy area in which we live for a quiet area <u>having</u> high quality properties.

5a)   **Ur mhn qst s t qt th nzy ara n wch w liv f a qyt ara hvg hgh qlty proprtys.**

6)   Please send us as quickly as <u>possible</u> the <u>quality</u> quilts ordered as they <u>are</u> required urgently by a very querulous customer.

6a)   **Pls snd us as qkly as psbl th qlty qlts ordrd. Thy r rqrd urjntly bi a vry qrwlz cstmr.**

7)   It is questionable whether the quantities <u>of</u> equipment sent *to us* are quite <u>what</u> we ordered.

7a)   **It s qstnbl wthr th qntys v eqpm snt tus r qte wht w ordrd.**

8)   The quick witted author of the questionnaire quibbled a lot when we queried some of his questions.

8a)   **Th qk witd awthr v th qstnhr qbld a lot whn w qryd sm v hs qstns.**

9)   *We could not* quell the childrens excitement at seeing the Queen.

9a)   ***Wcdnt* qel th chldrns xytmnt at zg th Qn.**

10)   We enclose herewith a list of the queries in the quotations for this quarter.

10a)   ***Weh* a lst v th qrys n th qwtns f ths qrtr.**

11)   The question is whether the manager will be quitting on quarter-day?

11a)   **Th qstn s wthr th mnjr wlb qtg on qrtr-dy?**

'SHORTS' (words in this category contain consonants only).
1.   quote/**qwt**, quoting/**qwtg**, quotation/**qwtn**
2.   quick/**qk**, quickly/**qkly**

GROUP R
Read and copy the 'Agiliwriting' shorthand exercises:

1)   The readers were encouraged to read the book on research in view of the reasonable review.

1a)   **Th rdrs wr ncrjd t rd th bwk on rsrch *nvwv* th rsnbl rvw.**

2)   Our recruitment programme has raised a reservoir of employable labour.

2a)   **Ur rcrwtm progrm hz rhzd a rsrvwr v mploybl lbr.**

3)   The rehabilitation of the ruins is quite remarkable.

3a)   **Th rhbltzn v th rwns s qte rmrkbl.**

4)   There will be a reappraisal of the rearrangements relating to the reappearance of the remaining readjustments.

4a)   ***Thrwlb* a ryprazl v th ryrnjms rlhtg t th ryprnz v th rmhng ryjstms.**

5)   *We will* refrigerate the refreshments reserved <u>for</u> those <u>taking part</u> in the rehearsals.

5a) **W*wl* rfrjrht th rfrshmnts rsrvd f thoz tkg prt n th rhrzls.**

6)   We <u>are</u> gr<u>ea</u>tly relieved by the relaxing <u>of</u> the remaining restrictions.

6a) **W r grhtly rlvd bi th rlaxg v th rmhng rstrcns.**

7)   The situation *will be* regularised when the manager recuperates <u>from</u> his illness <u>and</u> resumes his routine.

7a) **Th ztwzn *wlb* rglrzd whn th mnjr rcwprhts frm hs ilnz nd rzwms hs rwtn.**

8)   I hear <u>that</u> the restaurant nearby my residence <u>has</u> really <u>good</u> roast beef.

8a) **I hrh tht th rstrnt nrby mi rsdnz hz ryly gd rost bf.**

9)   *We will be* reappointing a new representative <u>to</u> reinforce our representation <u>in</u> the remote regions.

9a) **W*wlb* rypntg a nu rprsntv t rnfz ur rprsntzn n th rmot rjyns.**

10) *Can you please* return the register <u>of</u> records relating to the remittances <u>and</u> other remunerations.

10a) *Cnupls* **rtrn th rjstr v rcrds rlhtg t rmtnzs nd othr rmwnrhzns.**

11) *We will* reassess <u>and</u> review <u>the</u> proposed renovations <u>and</u> refurbishments <u>to</u> the restaurant's Rotisserie <u>room</u>.

11a) **W*wl* ryzs nd rvw th propzd rnovzns nd rfrbshmnts t th rstrnt's Rotzry rm.**

12) The rebellious rioters demanded a restitution <u>of</u> the rights removed <u>from</u> them by <u>the</u> ruthless ruler.

12a) **Th rblyz rytrs dmandd a rstwzn v th ryts rmvd frm thm bi th rwthls rwlr.**

13) *We can* recommend the readymade robes as they <u>are</u> realistically priced.

13a) *Wcn* rcmnd th rdymd rwbs as thy r rylstcly prcd.

14) The recovery <u>of</u> the <u>market</u> after the recent recession is remarkable.

14a) Th rcvry v th mrkt aftr th rsnt rzsn s rmrkbl.

15) It is reprehensible <u>how</u> the records *have been* repressed. There seems *to be* no rational reason for <u>not</u> revealing them <u>when</u> requested *to do so* by the Registrar.

15a) It s rprhnzbl hw th rcrds *hvbn* rprsd. Thr zms *tb* no raznl rsn f nt rvylg thm whn rqstd *tdoso* bi th Rjstrhr.

16) We realise the reimbursement <u>and</u> other remittances we <u>are</u> <u>to</u> receive will add <u>to</u> our revenue <u>for</u> *this year*. This means <u>that</u> our resources <u>will</u> <u>in</u> no <u>way</u> be restricted.

16a) W rylz th rmbrzmnt nd othr rmtnzs w r t rzv wl ad t ur rvnw f *ths yr*. Ths mns tht ur rsorzs wl n no wy b rstrctd.

17) I <u>hope</u> *you will* remember <u>to</u> reorganise <u>and</u> regularise the reinstatement <u>of</u> the rates <u>for</u> our various ranges.

17a) I hp *uwl* rmmbr t rorgnz nd rglrz th rnstatm v th rhts f ur vryz rnjs.

18) There is a restriction on the rents which *can be* obtained <u>for</u> rented accommodation <u>having</u> <u>small</u> rooms.

18a) Thr s a rstrcn on th rnts wch cnb obtnd f rntd acmdzn hvg sml rms.

19) *I have had* a really <u>good</u> look at the remainder <u>of</u> the Roumanian rollers for the Roundhouse and *it would be* realistic to keep them in reserve as a residue if any reconstruction is required.

19a) *Ihvhd* a ryly gd lwk at th rmhndr v th Rwmnyn rolrs f th Rwndhwz nd itwdb rylstc t kp thm n rsrv as a rzdw if ny rcnstrucn s rqrd.

'SHORTS' (words in this category contain consonants only).
Read and copy:

1.   road/**rd**'
2.   recover/**rcvr**, recovering/**rcvrng**, recovery/**rcvry**
3.   record/**rcrd**, recorder/**rcrdr**, recording/**rcrdg**
3.   regard/**rgrd**, regarded/**rgrdd**, regarding/**rgrdg**
4.   remark/**rmrk**, remarking/**rmrkg**, remarkabke/**rmrkbl**
5.   remove/**rmv**, removing/**rmvg**, removable/**rmvbl**
6.   repay/**rpy**, repaying/**rpyg**, repaid/**rpd**.

GROUP S

Read and copy the 'Agiliwriting' shorthand sentences:

1)   They say they are supremely satisfied with the secretarial services they
      have received. In their opinion, the typed schedules showed superior
      stenographic skills.

1a)   **Thy sy thy r zwprmly stsfd wth th scrtryl srvzs thy rzvd. N thyr opnyn,
      th typd shdwls shwd zwpryr stnogrfc skls.**

2)   We suppose it is safe to say that the straightforward socialist politician
      was speaking about sanctions and segregation policies.

2a)   **W spz it s sf t sy tht th strhtfwrd sozlst poltzn wz spkg abwt sancns nd
      sgrgzn polzys.**

3)   We suggest that the superintendent goes to the supermarket to investigate
      the suspicious shortages and seize the shoplifters. Surely other secure
      measures *could be* set-up!

3a)   **W sjst tht th suprntndnt* gwz t th suprmrkt* t nvstgt th suspshz
      shortjs nd zyz th shoplftrs. Zrly othr scwr mzrs *cdb* ztup!**
      ('super' can be 'zp' - 'supermarket = zpmrkt')

4)   It is no secret that science regards superstition and sentiment as superfi-
      cial.

4a)   **It s no scrt tht synz rgrds suprstzn* nd sntmnt as zprfzl*.**

      * zpstzn

5)   We <u>are</u> sincerely <u>sorry</u> about <u>the</u> sensitive situation <u>but</u> *it would not* be sensible <u>to</u> shoulder a show of strength *at the present time*. It is surely better to sustain <u>the</u> suspense until they surrender.

5a) **W r snzrly sry abwt th znstv ztwzn but *itwdntb* znzbl t shwldr a shw v strnth *athprsntm*. It s zrly btr t sustn th suspnz untl thy srndr.**

6)   We <u>are</u> sure *they will be* <u>very</u> satisfied with the simplicity <u>of</u> the suede leather samples sent to them.

6a) **W r zr *thywlb* vry stsfd wth th zmplzty v th swad lthr smpls snt t thm.**

7)   It seems *to us that* <u>the</u> <u>sooner</u> the scheme <u>for</u> substantial subsidisation of the schools situated in this section <u>of</u> the <u>country</u> <u>is</u> sanctioned, the <u>sooner</u> *we will* see a satisfactory standard.

7a) **It zms tus tht th snr th scm f sbstnzl sbsdzn v th scls ztwtd n ths scn v th cntry s sancnd, th snr *wwl* z a stsfctry stndrd.**

8)   The senior salesmen <u>have</u> satisfactorily <u>made</u> a great <u>saving</u> <u>for</u> us in applying a surcharge on all saleable <u>goods</u> shipped during this session.

8a) **Th znr zlsmn' hv stsfctrly md a grht svg f us n aplyg a srchrj on al zlbl gds shpd drng ths zsn.**

9)   The wholesaler *will be* <u>supplying</u> separates in all sizes. It seems *to us* after looking at the samples sent <u>that</u> the simpler shirts and silk blouses <u>are</u> more likely to suit our shoppers.

9a) **Th whlzlr *wlb* splyg sprhts n al szs. It zms *tus* aftr lwkg at th smpls snt tht th zmplr shrts nd slk blwzs r mor lkly t zwt ur shoprs.**

10) *I am* sincerely <u>sorry</u> <u>that</u> his shipment of standardised stocks of stereophonic speakers has <u>caused</u> something of a sensation this season. Someone <u>should</u> see him straight away and sound him out on his strategy <u>for</u> the next session.

10a) ***Im* snzrly sry tht hs shpm v th stndrdzd stoks v stryfonc spkrs hz czd smthng v a znzsn ths szn. Smwn shd zwnd hm ot on hs stratjy f th nxt zsn.**

11) The set-up on site to settle the settlers into the settlement is very supportive. They <u>are</u> searching <u>for</u> <u>ways</u> to overcome the shortage of supplies.

12a) **Th ztup on syt t ztl th ztlrs nto th ztlmnt s vry zportv. Thy r srchg f wys t ovrcm th svyr shortj v splys.**

13) The supervisor said he <u>was</u> <u>sorry</u> <u>that</u> the services *had been* suspended <u>for</u> the second time running. He <u>assured</u> us the <u>company</u> were <u>making</u> strenuous efforts <u>to</u> sustain a better standard by preventing further stoppages <u>and</u> shutdowns.

13a) **Th suprvzr zd h wz sry tht th srvzs *hdbn* suspndd f th scnd tym run'g. H azrd us th cmpny wr mkg strnwz efrts t sustn a btr stndrd bi prvntg frthr stopjs nd shutdwns.**

14) *I will be* staying with my sister at the seaside <u>this</u> summer. I enjoy swimming <u>in</u> the sea, *as well as* <u>country</u> walks so *I must not* forget my sensible walking shoes, especially as <u>her</u> house <u>is</u> situated <u>some</u> <u>way</u> off <u>from</u> the station.

14a) **Iwlb styg wth my sstr at th z'sd ths sumr. I njy swmg n th z', *aswls* cntry wlks so *Imznt* fgt mi znzbl wlkg zhws, espzly as hr hwz s ztwtd sm wy ov frm th stazn.**

15) The secondhand clothing shop sells shop-soiled samples <u>of</u> superior quality <u>and</u> if one is <u>not</u> too selective *it is* possible <u>to</u> buy <u>some</u> simply stunning styles.

15a) Th scndhnd clwthg shop sls shopzwld smpls v zwpryr qlty nd if wn s nt t' slctv, *its* psbl t by sm zmply stun'g styls.

'SHORTS' (words in this category contain consonants only.)
Read and copy:

1. since/**znz**, some/**sm**, something/**smthg**, someone/**smwn**
2. save/**sv**, saving/**svg**, saver/**svr**
3. sorry/**sry**, sell/**sl**, sale/**zl**, sample/**smpl**
4. second/**scnd**, secondhand/**scndhnd**
5. see/**z**, sea/**z'**, seen/**zn**, seeing/**zg**, saw/**zw**
6. say/**sy**, saying/**syg**, soon/**sn**
6. side/**sd**, said/**zd**
7. stay/**sty**, step/**stp**, still/**stl**

GROUP T
Read and copy the 'Agiliwriting' shorthand sentences:

1) The transport <u>company</u> testified <u>that</u> <u>they</u> <u>had</u> transferred the missing televisions.

1a) Th trnzpt cmpny tstfd tht thy hd trnzfrd th mzg tlvzns.

2) The test on Tuesday <u>was</u> time consuming, tedious, and tiresome. The main trouble being the technical terminology. Tempers were terrible.

2a) Th tst on Twsdy wz tym cnzmg, tdyz, nd tyrsm. Th mhn trwbl bng th tcncl trmnljy. Tmprs wr trbl.

3) The <u>trader</u> travelled throughout the territory <u>to</u> tell <u>them</u> about the new technology in telexes <u>and</u> telephones.

3a) Th trdr trvld thrwot th trtory t tl thm abwt th nu tcnljy n tlxs nd tlfns.

4) We thought the tactics <u>of</u> the treasurer <u>in</u> the transaction <u>were</u> well tymd.

4a) W thawt th tactcs v th trzrhr n th trnzcn wr wel tymed.

5) The tentative arrangements <u>made</u> concerning the tuition <u>and</u> training <u>of</u> teachers <u>is</u> tolerable.

5a) **Th tntv arnjmnts md cnsrng th twzn nd trhng v tchrs s tolrbl.**

6) We think the terms <u>of</u> trade <u>of</u> the typesetting <u>company</u> *will be* of tremendous value. There is <u>some</u> touching up *to be* <u>done</u> <u>to</u> the transcription <u>of</u> the typed terminology.

6a) **W thnk th trms v trd v th typztg cmpny *will be* v trmndwz vlw. Thr s sm twchg up tb dn t th trnzcrpn v th typd trmnljy.**

7) *We thank you* <u>for</u> sending us the taxation tables today, *as well as* the details of turnover <u>for</u> the last twelve months. It looks as though things need tightening up.

7a) ***Wtnku* f sndg us th txzn tbls tdy, *aswls* th dtls v trnovr f th lzt twlv mnths. It lwks as tho thngs nyd tytng up.**

8) We <u>are</u> taking over the offices in town on a temporary basis <u>from</u> tomorrow. I have bought a season ticket as I shall be travelling by train.

8a) **W r tkg ovr th ofzs on a tmprhry bzs frm tmorw. Ihv bawt a szn tkt as Ishlb trvlg bi trhn.**

9) It <u>was</u> a thrilling <u>and</u> tantalising theatrical performance <u>and</u> we <u>are</u> treating our friends <u>to</u> tickets <u>for</u> next Thursday's show.

9a) **It wz a thrilg nd tntlzg thytrcl prfmnz nd w r trtg ur frnds t tkts f nxt Thrsdy's shw.**

10) The terrorisation <u>of</u> the people living <u>in</u> the territory is terrifying. The terrorists *must be* brought <u>to</u> trial.

10a) **Th trorzn v th ppl livg n th trtry s trfyg. Th trorsts *mzb* brawt t tryl.**

11) I became timid about dieting <u>when</u> I saw the sausages <u>and</u> beans <u>in</u> a tempting thick tomato sauce.

11a) **I bcam tmd abwt dytg whn I zw th zwzjs nd bns n a tmptg thk tmto zwz.**

12)   I telephoned the retailer <u>to</u> tell <u>him</u> <u>that</u> the twenty special thick Terry towels <u>and</u> other toiletries required <u>are</u> being sent on <u>to</u> him by tonight's train. He had threatened to terminate trading *with us* unless we arranged <u>for</u> their urgent transport.

12a) **I tlfnd th rtlr t tel hm tht th twnty spzl thik Tery twls nd othr twltrys rqrd r bng snt on t hm bi tnyt's trhn. H hd thretnd t trmnht trdg *wthus* unls w arnjd f thyr urjnt trnzpt.**

13)   I thought the tax tables were terribly complicated. *I will* <u>have</u> <u>to</u> <u>take</u> the time next Tuesday <u>to</u> thoroughly study them.

13a) **I thawt th tx tbls wr trbly cmplctd. Iwl hv t tk th tym nxt Twsdy t thorwly study thm.**

14)   *I will be unable* <u>to</u> obtain the tickets <u>for</u> Taiwan <u>and</u> Thailand through my usual travel agents as <u>they</u> <u>have</u> just been taken over.

14a) **I*wlbunbl* to obtn th tkts f Tywn nd Tylnd thru mi uzwl trvl ajnts as thy hv jst bn tkn ovr.**

'SHORTS' (words in this category contain consonants only.)
Read and copy:

1.   take/**tk**, taking/**tkg**, takeover/**tkovr**
2.   table/**tbl**, tablet/**tblt**
3.   thank/**tnk**, thanking/**tnkg**
4.   the/**th**, there/**thr**, therefore/**thrfr**, these/**thz**, this/**ths**,
5.   to/**t**, too/**t'**, two/**tw**, towards/**twrds**
6.   trade/**trd**, trading/**trdg**, trader/**trdr**
7.   travel/**trvl**, travelling/**trvlg**, traveller/**trvlr**
8.   till/**tl**, total/**ttl,** toward/**twrd**, today/**tdy**

GROUP U

Read and copy the 'Agiliwriting' shorthand sentences:

1)   We <u>must</u> undertake <u>to</u> understand the underlying reasons <u>for</u> unemployment.

1a)   **W mz undrtk* t undrstnd th undrlyg rsns f unmploym.**

*('under' can be 'u' - 'undertake = u'tk')

2)   The University <u>has</u> a universal intake <u>of</u> foreign students.

2a)   **Th Unvrzty hz a unvrzl ntk v frn stwdnts.**

3)   Unofficial unpaid leave <u>is</u> <u>not</u> usually granted.

3a)   **Unofzl unpd lv s nt uzwly grntd.**

4)   It is <u>not</u> usual to underestimate the problems arising out <u>of</u> urbanisation.

4a)   **Its nt uzwl t u'estmt* th problms arzg ot v urbnzn.**

5)   It is useless <u>and</u> unnecessary <u>of</u> the unscrupulous usurper <u>to</u> undermine our unearthing <u>of</u> the undeniable facts.

5a)   **It s uzls nd unzsry v th unscrwplz usrpr t undrmyn ur unerthg v th undnybl fcts.**

6)   It is universally understood <u>that</u> a unilateral undertaking *would be* utterly unworkable <u>and</u> unacceptable.

6a)   **It s unvrzly undrstwd tht a unlatrl undrtkg wdb unwrkbl nd unacptbl.**

7)   The Unions united to uncover the reasons for the unfair and unique unemployment situation.

7a)   **Th Unyns unytd t uncvr th rsns f th unfhr nd unq unmploym ztwzn.**

GROUP V

Read and copy 'Agiliwriting' shorthand sentences:

1) The violent vandals viciously attacked their victims.

1a) **Th vylnt vndls vshzly atkd thyr vctms.**

2) *Could you please* vacate the premises in time for our vacation?

2a) ***Cdupls* vct th prems n tym f ur vczn?**

3) We are viewing the very valuable property today.

3a) **W r vwng th vry vlwbl proprty tdy.**

4) Without adequate ventilation the residents *will be* very vulnerable.

4a) **Wthot adqt vntlhzn th rsdnts wlb vry vulnrbl.**

5) The valuers have verified that their valuation is valid.

5a) **Th vlwrs hv vrfd tht thyr vlwzn s vld.**

6) Vegetarians will vouch for the value of a variety of vegetables and their versatility in the kitchen.

6a) **Vjtryns wl vwch f th vlw v a vryty v vjtbls nd thyr vrztlty n th kchn.**

7) The voice of the Vice-President throughout the victorious campaign was vibrant and vivacious. His vocation befits him.

7a) **Th vz v th VsPrsdnt thrwot th vctoryz cmpn wz vybrnt nd vvshz. Hs voczn bfts hm.**

8) The villager volunteered a vivid account of the accident to the visitor's vehicle and vouchsafed for the fact that it was caused by very poor visibility.

8a) **Th vljr volntrd a vvd acwnt v th acsdnt t th vztrs vhcl nd vwchsfd f th fct tht it wz czd bi vry por vzblty.**

'SHORTS':
Read and copy:

1. very/**vry**
2. village/**vlj**, villager/**vljr**
3. voice/**vz,** voicing/**vzg**
4. vice/**vs,** vice-vrsa/**vsvrza**

GROUP W

Read and copy the 'Agiliwriting' shorthand sentences:

1)   We <u>are</u> <u>sure</u> the increase in <u>wages</u> *will be* very welcome.

1a)   **W r zr th ncrz n wjs *wlb* vry wlcm.**

2)   *We would* <u>like</u> <u>to</u> know which weekend it <u>was</u> when the wholesaler <u>of</u> watches <u>was</u> waylaid on his <u>way</u> <u>to</u> the warehouse.

2a)   ***Wwd* lk t kno wch wknd it wz whn th whlzlr v wachs wz wylhd on hs wy t th whrhwz.**

3)   We <u>are</u> writing <u>to</u> *inform you* <u>that</u> we <u>are</u> willing <u>to</u> insure <u>your</u> workers on a worldwide basis when <u>they</u> work overseas.

3a)   **W r wrtg t nfmu tht w r wlg t nzr y wrkrs on a wrldwyd bzs whn thy wrk ovrzs.**

4)   *We will be* <u>very</u> pleased <u>to</u> welcome <u>you</u> this weekend <u>and</u> *we are sending you* our written confirmation.

4a)   ***Wwlb* vry plsd t wlcm u ths wknd nd *wrsndgu* ur wrtn cnfhmzn.**

5)   We <u>wonder</u> whether <u>they</u> <u>can</u> withstand the <u>long</u> walk <u>to</u> the railway station this winter.

5a)   **W wndr wthr thy cn wthstnd th lng wlk t th rhlwy stazn ths wntr.**

6)   We welcomed the <u>very</u> willing service <u>from</u> the waiters <u>and</u> waitresses at the restaurant last Wednesday all the while we were there.

6a)   **W wlcmd th vry wilg srvz frm th whtrs nd whtrzs at th rstrnt lzt Wnsdy al th wyl wwr thr.**

7)   The waterproofs wholesaler wishes us <u>to</u> visit his large warehouse <u>in</u> Winchester. As it *would be* worth our while *to do so*, we gave <u>him</u> our warranty <u>that</u> *we would* call on him <u>when</u> next <u>in</u> <u>his</u> vicinity.

7a)   **Th whlzlr n watrprwfs wshs u t vzt hs lrj wrhwz n Wnchstr. As *itwdb* wrth ur wyl *tdoso*, w gav hm ur wrnty tht *wwd* cl on hm whn nxt n hs vznty.**

8)   *We were* worried about the wellbeing <u>of</u> the working party in the worsening weather conditions.

8a)   **Wwr woryd abwt th welbng v th wrkg prty n th wrzng wethr cndzns.**

9)   In the winter weather it is wise <u>to</u> wear woollen underwear.

9a)   **N th wntr wethr it s wyz t wrh wln undrwr.**

10)   Weavers in the western part <u>of</u> the country weave wonderful worsted woollen waistcoats.

10a)   **Wvrs n th wstrn prt v th cntry wv wndrfl wrstd wln whstcts.**

11)   The woodworker lost the winder <u>of</u> his watch whilst working on the wooden window frames. *He does not* think a replacement is worthwhile as the watch is <u>not</u> worth <u>very</u> much.

11a)   **Th wdwrkr lost th wyndr v hs wach wylst wrkg on th wdn wndw frams. H *dznt* thnk a rplazm s wrthwyl as th wach s nt wrth vry mch.**

12)   I saw a wealth <u>of</u> wonderful plants in the gardens by the waterside, especially, wisterias, white daises and willows.

12)   **I zw a wlth v wndrfl plnts n th grdns bi th wtrsd, espzly, wstrys, wyt dhzys nd wlws.**

13)   On Wednesday I went <u>to</u> the wholesalers as I wished <u>to</u> see <u>some</u> cheap washing machines <u>and</u> wardrobes.

13a)   **On Wnsdy I wnt t th whlzlrs as I wshd t z sm chp wshg mshns nd wrdrwbs.**

14)   *We would* like <u>to</u> know the names and addresses <u>of</u> all witnesses <u>to</u> the accident <u>which</u> wrecked the vehicle when it <u>was</u> driven into the wall on Wednesday <u>of</u> last week.

14a)   **Wwd lk t kno th *nmsnadrzs* v al wtnzs t th acsdnt wch rekd th vhcl whn it wz drvn nto th wal on Wnsdy v lstwk.**

'SHORTS':
Read and copy:

1.   wage/**wj**
2.   wait/**wt**, waited/**wtd**, waiting/**wtg**
3.   want/**wnt**, was/**wz**, what/**wht**, with/**wth**, which/**wch**, we/**w**, when/**whn**
4.   were/**wr**, where/**whr**, whether/**wthr**
5.   walk/**wlk**, walking/**wlkg**
6.   water/wtr, watering/**wtrng**
7.   wholesale/**whlzl**, wholesalers/**whlzlr**, wholesaling/**whlzlg**
8.   would/**wd**, wood/**wd'**, woodworker/**wdwrkr**
9.   write/**wrt**, writing/**wrtg**, written/**wrtn**

GROUP Y
Read and copy the 'Agiliwriting' shorthand sentences:

1)   Did the youth go <u>to</u> the builder's yard yesterday?

1a)   **Dd th ywth go t th bldr's yrd ystrdy?**

2)   <u>They</u> say there <u>was</u> a great yield <u>from</u> the crops *this year*.

2a)   **Thy sy thr wz a grht yld frm th crops *thsyr*.**

3)   I understand <u>that</u> <u>you</u> <u>are</u> bringing <u>your</u> youngster <u>to</u> the school admission interview.

3a)   **I undrstnd tht u r brngng y yngstr t th scl admzn ntrvw.**

4)   I always enjoy the youthful enthusiasm <u>of</u> the young.

4a)   **I alwys njy th ywthfl nthwzyzm v th yng.**

5)   Yet again we intend sailing the yacht out <u>to</u> sea.

5a)   **Yt agn w ntnd zlg th yht ot t z'.**

6)   The years soon pass; let us <u>hope</u> the *next year will be* more peaceful than the *last year*.

6a)   **Th yrs sn ps; lt us hp th *nxyr* wlb mor pzful than th lstyr.**

7)   *Could you please* <u>take</u> the younger children <u>to</u> the Zoological Gardens.

7a)   **Cdupls tk th yngr chldrn t th Zwljcl Grdns?**

8)   I saw the youth yesterday <u>and</u> he asked me <u>to</u> l*et you know* <u>that</u> *he had* a yearning <u>to</u> see the girl he met last year on <u>your</u> yacht.

8a)   **I zw th ywth ystrdy nd h askd m t *ltuno* tht *hhd* a yrng t z th grl h met lstyr on th yht.**

'SHORTS':
Read and copy:

1.   you/**u**, your/**y**, year/**yr**
2.   yet/**yt**

LISTS

PREFIXES

ACQ = AQ
1. acquaint/**aqnt,** acquainting/**aqntg,** acquaintance/**aqntnz**
2. acquit/**aqt,** acquitting/**aqtg,** acquittal/**aqtl,** acquisitive/**aqztv**
3. acquiesce/**aqyz,** acquisition/**aqszn**
4. acquire/**aqr,** acquiring/**aqrng,** acquirement/**aqrmnt.**

AERO = AR
1. aeroplane/**arpln,** aerobatics/**arbtcs**

AIR = AR
1. airfield/**arfld,** airport/**arpt,** airways/**arwys**

AU = AW
Apart from the commencing vowel, **all vowels are deleted** in words commencing with **'aw'.**

1. author/**awthr,** authorise/**awthrz,** authorising/**awthrzg,** authorisation/**awthrzn.**
2. auction/**awcn,** auctioneer/**awcnr.**
3. audible/**awdbl,** audience/**awdynz,** auditor/**awdtr,** audition/**awdzn,** auditorium/**awdtrym*.**
4. Autumn/**Awtm,** automatic/**awtmtc,** automation/**awtmzn**
Exception:
dipthong 'iu' = 'y' is retained.

BE = B

1. become/**bcm**, becoming/**bcmg**, became/**bcam**
2. been/**bn**, being/**bng**, begin/**bgn**, beginning/**bgng**
3. behind/**bhnd**, beside/**bsd**

BIO = BY

1. biology/**bylojy**, biologist/**bylojst**, biological/**bylojcl**, biochemist/**bycmst**, biochemistry/**bycmstry.**

CEL=SL

1. celebrate/**slbrht**, celebrating/**slbrhtg**, celebration/**slbrhzn**, celebrity/**slbrty.**

CEN=SN

1. censor/**snsor**, censorious/**snsoryz**, censorship/**snsorshp**, censure/**snzr**, census/**snss.**
2. centre/**sntr**, centenarian/**sntnryn**, centenary/**sntnry**, centennial/**sntnyl.**
3. centralise/**sntrlz**, centralising/**sntrlzg**, centralisation/**sntrlzn.**
4. centigrade/**sntgrhd**, centimetre/**sntmtr.**

CER=SR

1. certain/**srtn**, certificate/**srtfct**, certify/**srtfy**, certifying/**srfyg**, certification/**srtfczn**, certitude/**srtwd.**

CIR=SR

1. circle/**srcl**, circular/**srclr**, circulate/**srclht**, circulating/**srclhtg**, circulation/**srclhzn.**
2. circularise/**srclrz**, circularising/**srclrzg**, circularisation/**srclrzn.**

CIRCUM = SRCM

1. circumstance/**srcmstnz**, circumstantial/**srcmstnzl.**
2. circumference/**srcmfrnz**, circumspect/**srcmspct.**

COM = CM

All vowels 'e' and 'i' are **deleted** in words commencing with 'com' = 'cm'.
1. commit/**cmt**, committment/**cmtm**, committing/**cmtg**, committe/**cmty**.
2. complex/**cmplx**, complexity/**cmplxty**, complexion/**cmplxn**.
3 command/**cmand**, commanding/**cmandg**, commandment/**cmandm**.
4. commend/**cmnd**, commending/**cmndg**, commendment/**cmndm**.
5. commission/**cmzn**, commissioning/**cmzng**, commissioner/**cmznr**, commissionaire/**cmznhr**.

CON = CN

All the vowels 'e' and 'i' are **deleted** in words commencing with 'con = cn'.
1. contain/**cntn***, containing/**cntng**, container/**cntnr**
2. connect/**cnct**, connecting/**cnctg**, connection/**cncn**.
3. confide/**cnfd**, confiding/**cnfdg**, confidence/**cnfdnz**, confidential/**cnfdnzl**
4. concur/**cncr**, concurring/**cncrng**, concurrent/**cncrnt**, concurrence/**cncrnz**
*'tain = tn'

CONCOM = CNCM
1. concomitant/**cncmtnt**, concomitance/**cncmtnz**

COIN = CWN
1. coincide/**cwnsd**, coinciding/**cwnsdg**, coincidence/**cwnsdnz**, coincident/**cwnsdnt**

CO-OP = COP
1. co-operate/**coprht**, co-operating/**coprhtg**, co-operation/**coprhzn**

CO-ORD = CORD
1. co-ordinate/**cordhnt**, co-ordinating/**cordnhtg**, co-ordination/**cordnhzn**

DE = D, DECOM = DCM, DECON = DCN
1. decompress/**dcmprs**, de/compose/**dcmpz**, decontaminate/**dcntmnht**, decongest/**dcnjst***
*Soft 'g' = 'j'

DES = DZ

1. despair/**dzpr**, desperate/**dzprht**, desperation/**dzprhzn**
2. despite/**dzpyt**, despicable/**dzpcbl**, despondant/**dzpondnt**

DEST = DST

1. destroy/**dstry**, destruction/**dstrucn**.
2. destiny/**dstny**, destined/**dstnd**, destination/**dstnhzn**.
Exception 'deserve = dsrv' (serve = srv)

DIA = DY

1. dial/**dyl**, dialling/**dylg**.
2. diabetic/**dybtc**, diagnosis/**dygnoss**, diagnostic/**dygnostc**.
3. dialect/**dylct**, dialogue/**dylog**, diametrical/**dymtrcl**, diatribe/**dytryb**.
4. diagram/**dygrm**, diametrical/**dymtrcl**, dialect/**dylct**, diabolical/**dybolcl**

DIS = DS

1. discharge/**dschrj**, discharging/**dschrjg**, dischargeable/**dschrjbl**.
2. disconnect/**dscnct**, disconnecting/**dscnctg**, disconnection/**dscncn**.
3. disturb/**dstrb**, disturbed/**dstrbd**, disturbing/**dstrbg**, disturbance/**dstrbnz**.
4. discuss/**dscuz**, discussing/**dscuzg**, discussion/**dscuzn**
5. disabled/**dsabld**, disability/**dsablty**.
6. disadvantage/**dsadvntj**, disadvantageous/**dsadvntjyz**.
7. disappear/**dsapr**, disappearing/**dsaprng**, disappearance/**dsaprnz**.
8. dislocate/**dsloct**, dislocating/**dsloctg**,
   dislocation/**dsloczn**.
9. disqualify/**dsqlfy***, disqualifying/**dsqlfyg**, disqualification/**dsqlfczn**.
10. disorganise/**dsorgnz**, dis/organising/**dsorgnzg**, disorganisation/**dsorgnzn**
*'qu = q'

DISIN = DSN

1. disinfect/**dsnfct**, disinfecting/**dsnfctg**, disinfection/**dsnfcn**
2. disinterest/**dsntrst**, disinteresting/**dsntrstg**
3. disintegrate/**dsntgrht**, disintegrating/**dsntgrhtg**, disintegration/**dsntgrhzn**

DISCOM = DSCM

1. discomfort/**dscmft**, discomforting/**dscmftg**
2. discomposed/**dscmpzd**, discomposure/**dscmpzr**

DISCON = DSCN

1. discontinue/**dscntnw**, discontinuing/**dscntnwng**, discontinuation/
   dscntnwzn,
   discontin<u>uou</u>s/**dscntnwz***
2. discontent/**dscntnt**, discontentment/**dscntntm***

*'wing = **wng**'
* dipthong '**uou = w**'
* suffix 'ment = m'

DIV = DV

1. division/**dvzn**, divisional/**dvznl**
2. divide/**dvd**, dividing/**dvdg**, division/**dvzn**
3. diverge/**dvrj**, diverging/**dvrjg**, divergent/**dvrjnt**, divergence/**dvrjnz**.
4. divulge/**dvulj**, divulging/**dvuljg**, divulgement/**dvuljm**

EM = M (when followed by a consonant)

1. embody/**mbdy**, embodying/**mbdyg**, embodyment/**mbdym**
2. employ/**mploy**, employing/**mployg**, employment/**mploym**

EM = EM (when followed by a vowel)

1. emerge/**emrj**, emerging/**emrjg**, emergency/**emrjnzy**

EN=N - when followed by a consonant.

1. engineer/**njnr**, engineering/**njnrng**
2. engross/**ngroz**, engrossing/**ngrozg**, engrossment/**ngrozm**
3. enter/**ntr**, entry/**ntry**, entertain/**ntrtn**, entertaining/**ntrtng**, entertainment/
   ntrtnm.
4. entrant/**ntrnt**, entrance/**ntrnz**

EN = EN (when followed by a vowel)

1. energy/**enrjy**, energetic/**enrjtc**
2. enemy/**enmy**, enmity/**enmty**

EN = N (when prefixing a 'root word')

3. en/able/**nabl**, en/abling/**nablg**, en/ablement/**nablm**
4. en/act/**nact**, en/acting/**nactg**, en/actment/**nactm**

EX = X

1. excellent/**xlnt**, excellency/**xlnzy**
2. extreme/**xtrm**, extremely/**xtrmly**, extremity/**xtrmty**
3. exite/**xyt**, exiting/**xytg**, exitement/**xytm**
4. expect/**xpct**, expecting/**xpctg**, expectation/**xpctzn**
5. expedite/**xpdyt**, expediting/**xpdytg**, expedition/**xpdzn**, expeditious/**xpdshz**
6. expend/**xpnd**, expending/**xpndg**, expensive/**xpnzv**

FOR = F

1. forbade/**fbad**, forbear/**fbr**, forbid/**fbid**,
    forgive/**fgv**, forego/**fgo**, foregone/**fgn**, foreground/**fgrwnd**,
2. formal/**fml**, formalise/**fmlz**, formalising/**fmlzg**,
    formalisation/**fmlzn**, formality/**fmlty**.
3. fortunate/**ftnht**, fortune/**ftwn**, fortnight/**ftnyt**,
    fthwth/**fthwth**

Exceptions:-

FOR = FOR :

4. forfeit/**forft**, forfeiting/**forftg**, forfeiture/**forftur**
    forge/**forj**, forklift/**forklft**, fort/**fort**,
    fortify/**fortfy**, fortification/**fortfczn**, fortress/**fortrz**, forest/**forst**,

GEN = JN

1. general/**jnrl**, generlise/**jnrlz**, generalising/**jnrlzg**,
    generalisation/**jnrlzn**.
2. generous/**jnrwz**, genius/**jnyz**, genial/**jnyl**, gentle/**jntl**.

GUAR = GR

1. guarantee/**grnty**, guaranteed/**grntyd**, guaranteeing/**grntyg**, guarantor/**grntr**.

IM = M (when followed by a consonant)

1. imply/**mply**, implying/**mplyg**, implicate/**mplct**,
    implicating/**mplctg**, implication/**mplczn**.
2. impinge/**mpnj**, impingingM/**mpnjg**, impingement/**mpnjm**
3. improve/**mprv**, improving/**mprvg**, improvement/**mprvm**

IM = IM (when followed by a vowel)

1. immediate/**imdyt**, immediately/**imdytly**
2. imitate/**imtt**, imitating/**imttg**, imitation/**imtzn**

IN = N

1. inactive/**nactv**, inaction/**nacn**
2. inefficient/**nefznt**, inadequate/**nadqt**
3. inequable/**neqbl**, inequality/**neqlty**
4. invest/**nvst**, inviting/**nvtg**, invitation/**nvtzn**
5. invest/**nvst**, investing/**nvstg**, investment/**nvstm**
6. investigate/**nvstgt**, investigating/**nvstgtg**, investigation/**nvstgzn**

INNO = INO
INNU = INW

1. innocent/**inosnt**, innocence/**inosnz**
2. innumerate/**inwmrht**, inumerating/**inwmrhtg**, inumeration/**inwmrhzn**
3. innuendo/**inwndo**

INCOM=NCM

1. incomplete/**ncmplt**, incompetent/**ncmptnt**, incompetence/**ncmptnz.**
2. incompatible/**ncmpatbl**, incompatibility/**ncmpatblty**
3. incommensurate/**ncmnzrht**, incommensurable/**ncmnzrbl**

INCON=NCN

1. inconsequent/**ncnsqnt**, inconsequential/**ncnsqnzl**
2. inconsiderate/**ncnsdrht**, inconsiderable/**ncnsdrbl**
3. inconclusive/**ncnclwzv**, inconceivable/**ncnzvbl**

INDEM = NDM

1. indemnify/**ndmnfy**, indemnification/**ndmnfczn**, indemnity/**ndmnty.**

INDIS = NDS

1. indiscreet/**ndscrt**, indiscretion/**ndscrzn**
2. indisposed/**ndspzd**, indisposition/**ndspzn**

IRRE=IR

1. irrecoverable/**ircvrbl**, irremovable/**irmvbl**, irreparable/**irprhbl**, irredeemable/**irdmbl**, irremediable/**irmdybl**, irremissible/**irmsbl**.
2. irrelevant/**irlvnt**, irregular/**irglr**, irregularity/**irglrty**, irrational/**iraznl**
3. irrepressible/**irprsbl**, irreproachable/**irprwchbl**, irresponsible/**irsponsbl**, irretrievable/**irtrvbl**, irreverence/**irvrnz**, irreversible/**irvrzbl**.

IRRI = IRY

1. irrigate/**irygt**, irrigating/**irygtg**, irrigation/**irygzn**
2. irritate/**irytt**, irritating/**iryttg**, irritation/**irytzn**

INEX = NX

1. inexperience/**nxprynz**, inexcusable/**nxcwzbl**, inexpensive/**nxspnzv**, inexplicable/**nxplcbl**, inexpressible/**nxprsbl**.

INTER = NTR

1. interval/**ntrvl**, intervene/**ntrvn**, intervening/**ntrvng**, intervention/**ntrvnzn**.
2. interchange/**ntrchnj**, intercommunicate/**ntrcmwnct**, interconnect/**ntrcnct**, interdependent/**ntrdpndnt**.
3. interim/**ntrm**, interested/**ntrstd**, interesting/**ntrstg**, interfere/**ntrfr**, interfering/**ntrfrng**, interference/**ntrfrnz**.
4. intermediate/**ntrmdyt**, intermediary/**ntrmdyry**, internal/**ntrnl**, international/**ntrnznl**, interpret/**ntrprt**, interpreter/**ntrprtr**, interpretation/**ntrprtzn**.

MACH = MSH

1. machine/**mshn**, machinery/**mshnry**, machinist/**mshnst**, machination/**mshnhzn**

MAG = MG

1. magnify/**mgnfy**, magnifying/**mgnfyg**, magnification/**mgnfczn**, magnificent/**mgnfsnt**.

MALA = MLA

1. maladjusted/**mlajstd**, malaria/**mlara**, malediction/**mladcn**, malefactor/**mlafctr**.

MECH = MC
1. mechanical/**mcncl**, mechanism/**mcnsm**, mechanise/**mcnz**, mechanising/**mcnzg**, mechanisation/**mcnzn**.

MEM = MM
1. memo/**mmo**, memorandum/**mmrndm**, memory/**mmry**, memorable/**mmrbl**, memorise/**mmrz**,
memorising/**mmrzg**, memorisation/**mmrzn**.

MIN = MN
1. minister/**mnstr**, ministry/**mnstry**, ministration/**mnstrhzn**, ministerial/**mnstryl**

MISS = MS
1. miss/**ms**, misuse/**msuz**, misusage/**msuzj**, misusing/**msuzg**, misunderstand/**msundrstnd**, misunderstanding/**msundrstndg**.
2. misapplied/**msaplyd**, misapplying/**msaplyg**, misapplication/**msaplczn**, misalliance/**msalynz**.

MISCON = MSCN
1. misconception/**mscnzpn**, misconstrue/**mscnstrw**, misconduct/**mscnduct**.

MISIN = MSN
1. misinterpret/**msntrprt**, misinterpretation/**msntrprtzn**, misinterpreting/**msntrprtg**, misinformed/**msnfmd**.

MISS/MS = MS
1. miss/**ms**, missing/**msg**, miscount/**mscwnt**, missile/**msyl**, mistress/**mstrz**.

MONO = MNO
1. monopoly/**mnoply**, monoplise/**mnoplz**, monopolising/**mnoplzg** monopolisation/**mnoplzn**.
2. monotony/**mnotny**, monotonous/**mnotnwz**.

NEO = NY
1. neoclassic/**nyclzc**, neolithic/**nylthc**, neologism/**nylojsm**.

NON = NN

1. non-aliance/**nnalynz**, non-aggression/**nnagrzn**, non-application/**nnaplczn**, non-attendance/**nnatndnz**, non-essential/**nnesnzl**, non-economic/**nnecnomc**, non-efficient/**nnefznt**, non-exchangeable/**nnxchnjbl**. non-believer/**nnblvr**, non-certified/**nnsrtfd**, non-certification/**nnsrtfczn**, non-chargeable/**nnchrjbl**, non-classifiable/**nnclzfybl**, non-habitable/**nnhbtbl**.
2. non-operational/**nnoprhznl**, non-negotiable/**nnngozbl**, non-occupational/**nnocpznl**.
3. nonsense/**nnsnz**, nonsensical/**nnsnzcl**, nonentity/**nnenty**, nondescript/**nndscrpt**.

PARA = PRH

1. parade/**prhd**, parading/**prhdg**, paradise/**prhdz**, parallel/**prhll**, paramount/**bprhmwnt**, parameter/**prhmtr**, parapet/**prhpt**, paraphrase/**prhfraz**, paraphernalia/**prhfrnla**.

PER = PR, PUR = PR

1. perfect/**prfct**, perfection/**prfcn**, ercent/**prznt**, perform/**prfm**, performance/**prfmnz**, performer/**prfmr**.
2. purpose/**prpz**, purchase/**prchz**, purchaser/**prchzr**, purchasing/**prchzg**.

PRE = PRY - 'long sound' as in 'preen', applied to 'root words'.

1. pre/caution/**pryczn**, pre/decease/**prydzys**, pre/deceasing/**prydzysg**, pre/determine/**prydtrmn**, pre/disposition/**prydspzn**, pre/meditate/**prymdtt**, pre/meditating/**prymdttg**, pre/meditation/**prymdtzn**.

PREA = PRY

1. preadvice/**prydvz**, prearrange/**pryrnj**, prearranging/**pryrnjg**, prearrangement/**pryrnjm**.

PH = F

1. photo/**fto**, photography/**ftogrfy**, prhotographer/**ftogrfr**, phone/**fn**, phonograph/**fnogrf**, phonetic/**fnetc**.

PHY = F

1. physique/**fzq**, physical/**fzcl**, physician/**fzsn**.

PRO = PRO

1. profess/**profz**, professing/**profzg**, profession/**profzn**, professional/**profznl**.
2. programme/**progrm**, programming/**progrmg**, programmer/**progmr**.
3. promote/**promt**, promoting/**promtg**, promotion/**promzn**, promotional/**promznl**.
4. promise/**proms**, promises/**proms'**, promising/**promsg**
5. propose/**propz**, proposing/**propzg**, proposition/**propzn**.

PSYCH = SYC

1. psychiatrist/**syctrst**, psychiatrical/**sycytrcl**, psychological/**sycljcl**, psychology/**sycljy**.

QU = Q

1. qualify/**qlfy**, qualifying/**qlfyg**, qualification/**qlfczn**
2. quality/**qlty**, qualitative/**qltv**
3. quit/**qt**, quitting/**qtg**, quittal/**qtl**, quittance/**qtnz**
4. quick/qk, quickly/qkly, quicker/**qkr**
5. quorum/**qorm**, queue/**qw**, queen/**qn**.

QU = QW

Exception
1. quote = **qwt**, qoutation = **qwtn**

RE - RE

1. re-enter = **rentr**, re-engage = **rengj**

RE - EX = RX

1. re-examine/**rxmn**

RE = R

1. re-let/rlt (**let = lt**)
2. repair/**rpr**, repairing/**rprng**, reserve/**rsrv** reserving/**rsrvg**, remain/**rmhn**,
3. remaining/**rmhng**, remainder/**rmhndr**, remind/**rmnd**,
4. reminding/**rmndg**, reminder/**rmndr**.

REA = RY

1. rearise/**ryrz**, rearising/**ryrzg**
2. rearrange/**ryrnj**, rearranging/**ryrnjg**, rearrangement/**ryrnjm**
3. reappraise/**rypraz**, reapraising/**rypraszg**, reapraisement/**ryprazmnt**
4. reaportion/**ryporzn**, reaportioning/**ryporzng**, reaportionment/**ryporznm**

REIM = RM

1. reimburse/**rmbrz**, reimbursing/**rmbrzg**, reimbursement/**rmbrzmnt**.

REIN = RN

1. reinforce/**rnfz**, reinforcing/**rnfzg**, reinforcement/**rnfzmnt**
2. reinstate/**rnstat**, reinstating/**rnstatg**,   reinstatement/**rnstatm**

RECOG = RCG

1. recognise/**rcgnz**, recognising/**rcgnzg**, recognition/**rcgnzn**.

RECOM=RCM

1. recommend/**rcmnd**, recommending/**rcmndg**, recommendation/**rcmndzn**
2. recompense/**rcmpnz**, recompensing/**rcmpnzg**.

RECON = RCN

1. reconcile/**rcnzl**, reconciling/**rcnzlg**, reconciliation/**rcnzlyzn**
2. recondition/**rcndzn**, reconnaissance/**rcnhsnz**, reconnoitre/**rcnwtr**.

RE-O = RO

1. re-occur/**rocr**, re-occurring/**rocrng**, re-occurence/**rocrnz**
2. re-occupy/**rocpy**, re=occupying/**rocpyg**, re-occupation/**rocpzn**
3. re-open/**ropn**, re-opening/**ropng**
4. re-operate/**roprht**, re-operating/**roprhtg**, re-operation/**roprhzn**
5. re-organise/**rorgnz**, re-organising/**rorgnzg**, re-organisation/**rorgnzn**
6. re-order/**rordr**, re-ordering/**rordrng**

RE-U = RU

1. reunion/**runyn**

SUB = SB

1. subscribe/**sbscrb**, subscribing/**sbscrbg**, subscription/**sbscpn**
2. subject/**sbjct**, subjecting/**sbjctg**, subjection/**sbjcn**
3. subjugate/**sbjwgt**, subjugating/**sbjwgtg**, subjugation/**sbjwgzn**
4. subside/**sbsd**, subsiding/**sbsdg**, subsidence/**sbsdnz**
5. subsidise/**sbsdz**, subsidising/**sbsdzg**, subsidisation/**sbsdzn**
6. submerge/**sbmrj**, submerging/**sbmrjg**, submergence/**sbmrjnz**

SUPER = SUPR or ZP

1. superabundant/**suprabundnt/zp**abundnt,
   supermarket/**suprmrkt/zp**mrkt
2. superficial/**suprfzl/zp**fzl,
   superfluous/**suprflwz/zp**flwz,
3. superintend/**suprntnd/zp**ntnd,
   superintendant/**suprntndnt/zp**ntndnt.

TRANS = TRNZ

1. transfer/**trnzfr**, transference/**trnzfrnz**, transcribe/**trnzcrb**, transcribing/
   trnzcrbg, transcription/**trnzcrpn**.
2. transpire/**trnzpr**, transit/**trnzt**, transition/**trnzsn**, transitional/**trnzsnl**.

UN - UN

1. uncertain/**unsrtn**, unconditional/**uncndznl**, unnatural/**unnhtrl**
   unoccupied/**unocpd**, unoccupational/**unocpznl**.
2. unreserved/**unrsrvd**, unremitting/**unrmtg**, unrelenting/**unrlntg**, unsaid/
   unzd,
   unsavoury/**unsavry**, unscrupulous/**unscrwplz**, unsettle/**unztl**, unsettling/
   unztlg.
3. unnecessary/**unzsry**, unnecessarily/**unzsrly**.

UNDER = UNDR or U'

1. undervalued/**undrvlwd/u'**vlwd
   undercharged/**undrchrjd/u'**chrjd
   understand/**undrstnd/u'**stnd
   understudy/**undrstudy/u'**study

UNIN = UNN

1. uninhibited/**unnhbitd**, uninhibiting/**unnhbtg**, uninhabitable/**unnhbtbl**.
2. uninterruption/**unntrupn**, uninviting/**unnvtg**.

VICE = VS

1. Vice-President/**Vsprsdnt**, Vice-Chairman/**Vschrmn**

YOUR = Y

1. yourself = **yslf**, yourselves = **yslvs**

LISTS

SUFFIXES & TERMINATIONS

Suffixes and **Terminations** are abbreviated as shown in the following examples:-

*Apart from the **commencing vowel,** all vowels **'e' and 'i'** are deleted in words containing an abbreviated prefix and/or suffix/termination.

*No double letters

1. **'sion'/'tion' = 'zn'**
    Examples:-

add/i/tion	add/i/**tion**	**adzn**
occasion	occa/**sion**	**oczn**
revision	re/vi/**sion**	**rvzn**

    *tional = 'znl'

intentional	in/ten/**tional**	**ntnznl**

    ('in = n')

emotional	e/mo/**tional**	**emoznl**
irrational	ir/ra/**tional**	**iraznl**

2. **'tion' following 'c' = 'cn'**
    Examples:-

election	ele/**ction**	**elcn**
erection	ere/**ction**	**ercn**
construction	con/stru/**ction**	**cnstrucn**
inspection	in/spe/**ction**	**nspcn**

    ('con = cn', 'in = n')

3.   'tion'/'tional' following 'p' = 'pn'/'pnl'
    Examples:-

assumption	assum/**ption**	**azmpn**

(assume = **azm**)

conscription	con/scri/**ption**	**cnscrpn**
inscription	in/scri/**ption**	**nscrpn**

('con = cn', 'in = n')

prescription	prescri/**ption**	**prscrpn**
subscription	sub/scri/**ption**	**sbscrpn**

('sub = sb)

exceptional	ex/ce/**ptional**	**xzpnl**

('ex = x')

*conscribe=cnsrcb, describe=dscrb, inscribe=nscrb, prescribe=prscrb, subscribe=sbscrb.

4.   **cession/session = 'zsn'**
    Examples:-

assession	a/**session**	**azsn**
concession	con/**cession**	**cnzsn**

('con = cn')

recession	re/**cession**	**rzsn**

5.   **possession = pzsn**

depossession	de/**possession**	**dpzsn**
repossession	re/**possession**	**rpzsn**

('de = d', 're = r')

6.   **'cess', 'sess' = zs**
    'cessing', 'sessing' = zsg
    Examples:-

access	ac/**cess**	**aczs**
accessing	ac/**cess**/ing	**aczsg**
assess	as/**sess**	**azs**
assessing	as/**sess**/ing	**azsg**

possess	pos/**sess**	**pzs**
possessing	pos/**sess**/**ing**	**pzsg**
recess	re/**cess**	**rzs**
recessing	re/**cess**/**ing**	**rzsg**
pro/cess	pro/**cess**	**prozs**
pro/cess/ing	pro/**cess**/**ing**	**prozsg**

('pro = pro')

7. **Plurals: Add 's'**
   Words ending with 's' = 'ss'.
   Examples:-

assess = **azs**	assesses = **azss**
access = **aczs**	accesses = **aczss**
possess = **pzs**	possesses = **pzss**
process = **prozs**	processes = **prozss**

8. **cessive/sessive = 'zsv'**
   Examples:-

concessive	con/**cessive**	**cnzsv**

   ('con = cn')

excessive	ex/**cessive**	**xzsv**

   ('ex = x')

recessive	re/**cessive**	**rzsv**
possessive	pos/**sessive**	**pzsv**

   *Note:

accessory	ac/**cess**/ory	**aczsry**
necessary	ne/**cess**/ary	**nzsry**
necessity	ne/**cess**/ity	**nzsty**

9. **'cision/sician/sition = 'szn'.**
   Examples:-

decision	de/**cision**	**dszn**
indecision	in/de/**cision**	**ndszn**
incision	in/**cision**	**nszn**

   ('de = d','in = n')

physician	phy/**sician**	**fszn**

   ('ph' = 'f')

musician	mu/**sician**	**mwszn**
recision	re/**cision**	**rszn**

10. The termination **'sition'** in the word **'position'** is abbreviated to **'zn'**.
Examples:-

position	po/**sition**	**pzn**
composition	com/**position**	**cmpzn**

(**'com = cm'**)

deposition	de/**position**	**dpzn**
exposition	ex/**position**	**xpzn**

(**'ex = x'**)

imposition	im/**position**	**mpzn**

(**'im' = 'm'**)

supposition	su/**position**	**spzn**

11. **pose = pz'**
Examples:-

compose	com/**pose**	**cmpz**
depose	de/**pose**	**dpz**
ex/pose	ex/**pose**	**xpz**

(**'ex = x'**)

impose	im/**pose**	**mpz**

(**'im = m'**)

propose	pro/**pose**	**propz**

(**'pro = pro'**)

reimpose	reim/**pose**	**rmpz**

(**'reim = rm'**)

suppose	sup/**pose**	**spz**

12. **'cide' 'side' = 'sd'**:-
Examples:-

aside	a/**side**	**asd**
decide	de/**cide**	**dsd**
reside	re/**side**	**rsd**

13. **'cise' 'size' = 'sz'**:-
Examples:-

concise	con/**cise**	**cnsz**

(**'con = cn'**)

criticise	cri/ti/**cise**	**crtsz**
exercise	ex/er/**cise**	**xrsz**

(**'ex = x'**)

incise	in/**cise**	**nsz**

(**'in = n'**)

precise	pre/**cise**	**prsz**

14. **'cede' 'ceed' 'ceding' 'ceeding' = 'zd' 'zdg'**
Examples:-

accede	ac/**cede**	**aczd**
acceding	ac/**ceding**	**aczdg**
concede	con/**cede**	**cnzd**
conceding	con/**ceding**	**cnzdg**
intercede	inter/**cede**	**ntrzd**
interceding	inter/**ceding**	**ntrzdg**

('inter = ntr')

proceed	pro/**ceed**	**prozd**
proceeding	pro/**ceeding**	**prozdg**

('pro = pro')

recede	re/**cede**	**rzd**
receding	re/**ceding**	**rzdg**

('re = r')

15. **'cial' and 'tial' = 'zl'**
Examples:-

social	so/**cial**	**sozl**
financial	fi/nan/**cial**	**fnanzl**
deferential	de/fer/en/**tial**	**dfrnzl**
partial	par/**tial**	**parzl**
substantial	sub/stan/**tial**	**sbstnzl**

('sub = sb')

16. **'cious' 'tious' = 'shz'**
Examples:-

conscious	con/**scious**	**cnshz**

('con = cn')

delicious	de/li/**cious**	**dlshz**
judicious	ju/di/**cious**	**jwdshz**
ambitious	am/bi/**tious**	**ambshz**
infectious	in/fec/**tious**	**nfcshz**

('in = n')

conscientious	con/scien/**tious**	**cnzynshz**
superstitious	su/per/sti/**tious**	**suprstshz***

('super = supr or 'zp' - 'superstitious = zpstshz')

17.   'cient' 'tient' = 'znt'
      Examples:-

efficient	ef/i/**cient**	**efznt**
deficient	de/fi/**cient**	**dfznt**
sufficient	suf/i/**cient**	**sfznt**
patient	pa/**tient**	**paznt**

18.   **'ment' is abbreviated to 'm' 'mental' to 'mntl' following a consonant.**
      Examples:-

excitement	exc/ite/**ment**	**xytm**

('**ex**' = '**x**')

engagement	en/gage/**ment**	**ngjm**

('**en** = **n**')

refurbishment	re/fur/bish/**ment**	**rfrbshm**
fundamental	funda/**mental**	**fundmntl**

19.   **Following the consonants 'r', 'ment = mntl':-**

deferment	de/fer/**ment**	**dfrmnt**
determent	de/ter/**ment**	**dtrmnt**
experiment	ex/per/i/**ment**	**xprmnt**
experimental	ex/per/i/**mental**	**xprmntl**

('**ex = x**')

20.   **'bate=bt' 'bating=btg' 'bation=bzn'**
      Examples:-

exacerbate	exacer/**bate**	**xasrbt**
exacerbating	exacer/**bating**	**xasbtg**
exacerbation	exacer/**bation**	**xasrbzn**
probate	pro/**bate**	**probt**
probation	pro/**bation**	**probzn**

('**pro** = **pro**')
*Note - abate=abht, debate=dbht, rebate=rbht

21. 'cate=ct' 'cating=ctg' 'cation=czn'
Examples:-

confiscate	con/fis/**cate**	**cnfsct**
confiscating	con/fis/**cating**	**cnfsctg**
confiscation	con/fis/**cation**	**cnfsczn**

('con = cn')

duplicate	dupli/**cate**	**dwplct**
duplicating	dupli/**cate**	**dwplctg**
duplication	dupli/**cation**	**dwplczn**

indicate	in/di/**cate**	**ndct**
indicating	in/di/**cating**	**ndctg**
indication	in/di/**cation**	**ndczn**

('in = n')

22. 'date=dt' 'dating=dtg' 'dation=dzn'
Examples:-

accommodate	accommo/**date**	**acmdt**
accommodating	accommo/**dating**	**acmdtg**
accommodation	accommo/**dation**	**acmdzn**

('commo = cm')

invalidate	in/vali/**date**	**nvldt**
invalidating	in/vali/**dating**	**nvldtg**
invalidation	in/vali/**dation**	**nvldzn**

('in = n')
*Note: 'date'='dt' 'dated = dtd' 'dating = dtg'

23. 'gate=gt' 'gating=gtg' 'gation=gzn'
Examples:-

aggregate	aggre/**gate**	**agrgt**
aggregating	aggre/**gating**	**agrgtg**
aggregation	aggre/**gation**	**agrgzn**
delegate	dele/**gate**	**dlgt**
delegating	dele/**gating**	**dlgtg**
delegation	dele/**gation**	**dlgzn**
instigate	in/sti/**gate**	**nstgt**
instigating	in/sti/**gating**	**nstgtg**
instigation	in/sti/**gation**	**nstgzn**

('in = n')

subjugate	sub/ju/**gate**	**sbjwgt**
subjugating	sub/ju/**gating**	**sbjwgtg**
subjugation	sub/ju/**gation**	**sbjwgzn**

('sub = sb')

propogate	pro/po/**gate**	**propgt**
propogating	pro/po/**gating**	**propgtg**
propogation	pro/po/**gation**	**propgzn**

('**pro = pro**)

24. '**late=lht**' '**lating=lhtg**' '**lation=lhzn**'
These terminations relate to 'Linked Consonants' -
(Refer to appropriate chapter).

**When the vowel 'u' precedes the consonant 'l' in a
word which contains the consonant 'h', the vowel 'u' is omitted.**

calculate	calcu/**late**	**clclht**
calculating	calcu/**lating**	**clclhtg**
calculation	calcu/**lation**	**clclhzn**
relate	re/**late**	**rlht**
relating	re/**lating**	**rlhtg**
relation	re/**lation**	**rlhzn**
regulate	regu/**late**	**rglht**
regulating	regu/**lating**	**rglhtg**
regulation	regu/**lation**	**rglhzn**

**The vowel 'u' is retained when words commence with a
vowel as in the following example:-**

emulate	emu/**late**	**emwlht**
emulating	emu/**lating**	**emwlhtg**
emulation	emu/**lation**	**enwlhzn**

*The long soft sound of 'u' as in 'tube' = 'w'

25. '**mate=mt**' '**mating=mtg**' '**mation=mzn**'
Examples:-

animate	ani/**mate**	**anmt**
animating	ani/**mating**	**anmtg**
animation	ani/**mation**	**anmzn**
approximate	approxi/**mate**	**aproxmt**
approximating	approxi/**mating**	**aproxmtg**
approximation	approxi/**mation**	**aproxmzn**
estimate	esti/**mate**	**estmt**
estimation	esti/**mating**	**estmtg**
estimation	esti/**mation**	**estmzn**

26.   'minate = mnht' 'minating = mnhtg' 'mination = mnhzn'
       Examples:-

exterminate	ex/ter/**minate**	**xtrmnht**
exterminating	ex/ter/**minating**	**xtrmnhtg**
extermination	ex/ter/**mination**	**xtrmnhzn**

('**ex = x**')

terminate	ter/**minate**	**trmnht**
terminating	ter/**minating**	**trmnhtg**
termination	ter/**mination**	**trmnhzn**

27.   'nate = nht 'nating = nhtg' 'nation = nhzn'
       Examples:-

co-ordinate	co-ordi/**nate**	**cordnht**
co-ordinating	co-ordi/**nating**	**cordnhtg**
co-ordination	co-ordi/**nation**	**cordnhzn**

('**co-or**')

designate	desig/**nate**	**dzgnht**
designating	desig/**nating**	**dzgnhtg**
designation	desig/**nation**	**dzgnhzn**

('**des = dz**')

28.   'pate = pt' 'pating =p tg' 'pation =p zn'
       Examples:-

anticipate	antici/**pate**	**antzpt**
anticipating	antici/**pating**	**antzptg**
anticipation	antici/**pation**	**antzpzn**
participate	partici/**pate**	**prtzpt**
participating	partici/**pating**	**prtzptg**
participation	partici/**pation**	**prtzpzn**

'**part = prt**'

29. **'sate = zt' 'sating = ztg' 'sation = zsn'**
Examples:-

compensate	com/pen/**sate**	**cmpnzt**
compensating	com/pen/**sating**	**cmpnztg**
compensation	com/pen/**sation**	**cmpnzsn**

('com = cm')

dispensate	dis/pen/**sate**	**dspnzt**
dispensating	dis/pen/**sating**	**dspnztg**
dispensation	dis/pen/**sation**	**dspnzsn**

('dis = ds')

30. **'tate = tt' 'tating = ttg' 'tation = tzn'**
Examples:-

agitate	agi/**tate**	**ajtt**
agitating	agi/**tating**	**ajttg**
agitation	agi/**tation**	**ajtzn**
commentate	commen/**tate**	**cmntt**
commentating	commen/**tating**	**cmnttg**
commentation	commen/**tation**	**cmntzn**

('com = cm')

imitate	imi/**tate**	**imtt**
imitating	imi/**tating**	**imttg**
imitation	imi/**tation**	**imtzn**

31. **'titive = tv'**
Examples:-

competitive	com/pe/**titive**	**cmptv**

('com = cm')

repetitive	repe/**titive**	**rptv**

32. **'vate = vt', 'vating = vtg', 'vation = vzn'**
Examples:-

aggravate	a/gra/**vate**	**agrvt**
aggravating	a/gra/**vat/ing**	**agrvtg**
aggravation	a/gra/**va/tion**	**agrvzn**
inovate	ino/**vate**	**inovt**
inovating	ino/**vating**	**inovtg**
inovation	ino/**vation**	**inovzn**

('in = in' when followed by a vowel)

renovate	re/no/**vate**	**rnovt**
renovating	reno/**vating**	**rnovtg**
renovation	reno/**vation**	**rnovzn**

*'rate=rht' 'rating=rhtg' 'ration=rhzn'
(These suffixes relate to **'Linked Consonants',** refer to the appropriate chapter)

33.   **'berate=brht' 'berating=brhtg' 'beration=brhzn'**
       Examples:-

deliberate	deli/**berate**	**dlbrht**
deliberating	deli/**berating**	**dlbrhtg**
deliberation	deli/**beration**	**dlbrhzn**
reverberate	rever/**berate**	**rvrbrht**
reverberating	rever/**berating**	**rvrbrhtg**
reverberation	rever/**beration**	**rvrbrhzn**

34. **'cerate=zrht' 'cerating=zrhtg' 'seration=zrhzn'**
     Examples:-

commiserate	com/mi/**serate**	**cmzrht**
commiserating	com/mi/**serating**	**cmzrhtg**
commiseration	com/mi/**seration**	**cmzrhzn**

     ('com = cm')

35. **'derate=drht' 'dering = drng' 'deration=drhzn'**

considerate	con/side/**rate**	**cnsdrht**
considering	con/side/**ring**	**cnsdrng**

     ('ring = rng')

consideration	con/side/**ration**	**cnsdrhzn**

     ('con = cn')
*Note: 'consider = cnsdr', 'considerable = cnsdrbl'

36.   **'ferate=frht' 'ferating=frhtg' 'feration=frhzn'**
       Examples:-

proliferate	pro/life/**rate**	**prolfrht**
proliferation	pro/life/**rating**	**prolfrhtg**
proliferation	pro/life/**ration**	**prolfrhzn**

     ('pro = pro')

37. **'gerate=jrht' 'gerating=jrhtg' geration=jrhzn'**

Examples:-

exaggerate	exagge/**rate**	**xajrht**
exaggerating	exagge/**rating**	**xajrhtg**
exaggeration	exagge/**ration**	**xajrhzn**

(**'ex = x'**)

38. **'merate=mrht' 'merating=mrhtg' 'meration=mrhzn'**
Examples:-

enumerate	enu/**merate**	**enwmrht**
enumerating	enu/**merating**	**enwmrhtg**
enumeration	enu/**meration**	**enwmrhzn**

39. **'perate=prht' 'perating=prhtg' 'peration=prhzn'**
'parate=prht' 'parating=prhtg' 'paration=prhzn'
'porate=prht' 'porating=prhtg' 'poration=prhzn'

Examples:-

co-operate	co-o**perate**	**coprht**
co-operating	co-o**perating**	**coprhtg**
co-operation	co-o**peration**	**coprhzn**

(**'co-op = cop'**)

exasperate	exas/**perate**	**xasprht**
exasperating	exas/**perating**	**xasprhtg**
exasperation	exas/**peration**	**xasprhzn**

(**'ex = x'**)

incorporate	in/cor/**porate**	**ncrprht**
incorporating	in/cor/**porating**	**ncrprhtg**
incorporation	in/cor/**poration**	**ncrprhzn**

(**'incor = ncr'**)

separate	se/**parate**	**sprht**
separating	se/**parating**	**sprhtg**
separation	se/**paration**	**sprhzn**
desperate	des/**perate**	**dzprht**
desperation	des/**peration**	**dzprhzn**

(**'des = dz'**)

40.   **'terate=trht' 'terating=trhtg' 'teration=trhzn'**
Examples:-

obliterate	obli/**terate**	**obltrht**
obliterating	obli/**terating**	**obltrhtg**
obliteration	obli/**teration**	**obltrhzn**
reiterate	rei/**terate**	**rytrht**
reiterating	rei/**terating**	**rytrhtg**
reiteration	rei/**teration**	**rytrhzn**

('rei' = 'ry')

41.   **'perable=prhbl' 'parable=prhbl' 'parative=prhtv' 'perative=prhtv'**
Examples:-

comparable	com/**parable**	**cmprhbl**
comparative	com/**parative**	**cmprhtv**

('com = cm')

imperative	im/**perative**	**mprhtv**

('imper = mpr')

operable	o/**perable**	**oprhbl**
operative	o/**perative**	**oprhtv**
separable	se/**parable**	**sprhbl**
inseparable	in/se/**parable**	**nsprhbl**

('in = n')

42.   **'rable=rbl' 'ring=rng'**
Examples:-

considerable	con/side/**rable**	**cnsdrbl**
considering	con/side/**ring**	**cnsdrng**

('con = cn', 'ring = rng')
Note: 'consider = cnsdr'

43.   **'dise=dz' 'dising=dzg' 'disation=dzn'**
Examples:-
grand = grand

aggrandise	agran/**dise**	**agrandz**
aggrandising	agran/**dising**	**agrandzg**
aggrandisation	agran/**disation**	**agrandzn**

liquid = lqd

liquidise	liqui/**dise**	**lqdz**
liquidising	liqui/**dising**	**lqdzg**
liquidisation	liqui/**disatio**	**lqdzn**

('qu = q')

subsidy = sbsdy

subsidise	sub/si/**dise**	**sbsdz**
subsidising	sub/si/**dising**	**sbsdzg**
subsidisation	sub/si/**disation**	**sbsdzn**

('sub = sb')

44. **'lise = lz' 'lising = lzg' 'lisation = lzn'**

Examples:-
material = mtryl

materialise	materia/**lise**	**mtrylz**
materialising	materia/**lising**	**mtrylzg**
materialisation	materia/**lisation**	**mtrylzn**

nation = nhzn
national = naznl

nationalise	nationa/**lise**	**naznlz**
nationalising	nationa/**lising**	**naznlzg**
nationalisation	nationa/**lisation**	**naznlzn**

real = ryl

realise	rea/**lise**	**rylz**
realising	rea/**lising**	**rylzg**
realisation	rea/**lisation**	**rylzn**

ration = razn

rationalise	rationa/**lise**	**raznlz**
rationalising	rationa/**lising**	**raznlzg**
rationalisation	rationa/**lisation**	**raznlzn**

special = spzl

specialise	specia/**lise**	**spzlz**
specialising	specia/**lising**	**spzlzg**
specialisation	specia/**lisation**	**spzlzn**

social = sozl

socialise	socia/**lise**	**sozlz**
socialising	socia/**lising**	**sozlzg**
socialisation	socia/**lisation**	**sozlzn**

45. 'mise=mz' 'mising=mzg' 'misation=mzn'

Examples:-
economy = ecnomy

economise	e/con/o/**mise**	**ecnomz**
economising	e/con/o/**mising**	**ecnomzg**
economisation	e/con/o/**misation**	**ecnomzn**

minimum = mnmm

minimise	mini/**mise**	**mnmz**
minimising	mini/**mising**	**mnmzg**
minimisation	mini/**misation**	**mnmzn**

46. 'nise = nz', 'nising = nzg', 'nition = nzn'

Examples:-

recognise	recog/**nise**	**rcgnz**
recognising	recog/**nising**	**rcgnzg**
recognition	recog/**nition**	**rcgnzn**

('**cog = cg**')

47. 'rise=rz' 'rising=rzg' 'risation=rzn'

Examples:-
regular = rglr

regularise	regula/**rise**	**rglrz**
regularising	regula/**rising**	**rglrzg**
regularisation	regula/**risation**	**rglrzn**

tender = tndr

tenderise	tende/**rise**	**tndrz**
tenderising	tende/**rising**	**tndrzg**
tenderisation	tende/**risation**	**tndrzn**

48. ' tise=tz' 'tising=tzg' 'tisation=tzn'

climate = clymt

acclimatise	acclima/**tise**	**aclymtz**
acclimatising	acclima/**tising**	**aclymtzg**
acclimatisation	acclima/**tisation**	**aclymtzn**

'**advertise = advrtz**'

49.   **'vise = vz', 'vising = vzg', 'vision = vzn'**
    Examples:-

supervise	super/**vise**	**suprvz/zpvz**
supervising	super/**vising**	**suprvzg/zpvzg**
supervision	super/**vision**	**suprvzn/zpvzn**

    ('super = supr/zp')

advise	ad/**vise**	**advz**
devise	de/**vise**	**dvz**
revise	re/**vise**	**rvz**
division	di/**vision**	**dvzn**
provision	pro/**vision**	**provzn**

    ('pro = pro')

50.   **'tain=tn' 'taining = tng', 'tainment = tnm'**
    Examples:-

ascertain	ascer/tain	**asrtn**
ascertaining	ascer/taining	**asrtng**
ascertainment	ascer/tainment	**asrtnm**
contain	con/tain	**cntn**
containing	con/taining	**cntng**
containment	con/tainment	**cntnm**
detain	de/**tain**	**dtn**
detaining	de/**tain/ing**	**dtng**
detainment	de/**tain/ment**	**dtnm**
pertain	per/**tain**	**prtn**
pertaining	per/**tain/ing**	**prtng**
pertainment	per/**tain/ment**	**prtnm**
retain	re/**tain**	**rtn**
retaining	re/**tain/ing**	**rtng**
retainment	re/**tain/ment**	**rtnm**

    *'**curtain = crtn', 'curtaining = crtng'**

51.   **'ing = g'**
    'ning' = 'n'g' to avoid identical abbreviations
    Examples:-

running = **run'g**	(rung = **rung**)
stun/ning = **stun'g**	(stung = **stung**)
thinning = **thn'g**	(thing = **thng**)
winning = **wn'g**	(wing = **wng**)

52. 'tail=tl' 'tailing = tlg' 'tailment = tlm'
     Examples:-

cur/tail	cur/**tail**	**crtl**
curtailing	cur/**tail**/**ing**	**crtlg**
curtailment	cur/**tail**/**ment**	**crtlm**
detail	de/**tail**	**dtl**
detailing	de/**tail**/**ing**	**dtlg**
entail	en/**tail**	**ntl**
entailing	en/**tail**/**ing**	**ntlg**

('en = n')

retail	re/**tail**	**rtl**
retailing	re/**tail**/**ing**	**rtlg**

'retailer = rtlr'

53. 'vail = vl' 'vailing = vlg' 'vailable = vlbl'
     Examples:-

avail	a/**vail**	**avl**
availing	a/**vail**/**ing**	**avlg**
available	a/**vail**/**able**	**avlbl**
prevail	pre/**vail**	**pryvl**
prevailing	pre/**vail**/**ing**	**pryvlg**

('pre = pry')

54. 'stitute' = 'stwt' stitution = stwzn
     Examples:-

constitute	con/**stitute**	**cnstwt**
consti tution	con/**stitution**	**cnstwzn**

('con = cn')

destitute	de/**stitute**	**dstwt**
destitution	de/**stitution**	**dstwzn**
institute	in/**stitute**	**nstwt**
institution	in/**stitution**	**nstwzn**

('in = n')

prostitute	pro/**stitute**	**prostwt**
prostitution	pro/**stitution**	**prostwzn**

('pro = pro')

55. 'titude' = twd'
     Examples:-

attitude	at/**titude**	**atwd**
altitude	al/**titude**	**altwd**
rectitude	rec/**titude**	**rctwd**

56. **'it' following a consonant = 't'.**
Examples:-

edit	ed/**it**	**edt**
emit	em/**it**	**emt**
omit	om/**it**	**omt**
permit	perm/**it**	**prmt**

('per = pr')

remit	rem/**it**	**rmt**
submit	sub/**mit**	**sbmt**

('sub = sb')

57. **'ring = rng'**
Examples:-

bettering	bette/**ring**	**btrng**
lettering	lette/**ring**	**ltrng**
rendering	rende/**ring**	**rndrng**

58. **'wing = wng'**
Examples:-

renewing	rene/**wing**	**rnwng**
reviewing	revie/**wing**	**rvwng**

59. **'low = lw':**
Examples:-

follow	fol/low	**folw**
hollow	hol/low	**holw**
shallow	shallow	**shalw**

60. **'row = rw':**
Examples:-

borrow	bor/row	**borw**
narrow	nar/row	**narw**
sorrow	sor/row	**sorw**

61. 'graph = grf', 'graphic = grfc', 'graphy = grfy',graphical = grfcl'
Examples:-

lithography	lith/o/**graphy**	**lthogrfy**
lithographical	lith/o/**graphical**	**lthogrfcl**
geography	geo/**graphy**	**jygrfy**
geo/graphical	geo/**graphical**	**jygrfcl**

('soft 'g' = 'j')

| photographic | pho/to/**graphic** | **ftogrfc** |
| photography | pho/to/**graphy** | **ftogrfy** |

('photo = fto')

62. 'ology = ljy', 'ological = ljcl'
Examples:-

| technology | tech/**no/logy** | **tcnljy** |
| technological | tech/**no/logical** | **tcnljcl** |

63. 'rable = rbl', 'table = tbl'
Examples:-

| vegetable | ve/ge/table | **vjtbl** |
| venerable | ve/ne/rable | **vnrbl** |

64. 'ded = dd', 'rer = rhr' or r''
Examples:-

| confide = **cnfd** | confi/ded = **cnfdd** |
| decide = **dsd** | deci/ded = **dsdd** |

bear = **bhr**	bea/rer = **bhrhr** or **bhr'**
fair = **fhr**	fai/rer = **fhrhr** or **fhr'**
near = **nr**	nea/rer = **nrhr** or **nr'**

LISTS

SHORTS

(Words in this category contain consonants only).

A

are	r
and	nd
any	ny
anybody	nybdy
anyone	nywn
anything	nythg
anywhere	nywhr
answer	nsr

B

bank	bnk
base	bz
basic	bzc
basically	bzcly
become	bcm
becoming	bcmg
behalf	bhf
be	b
being	bng
belong	blng
belonging	blngng
best	bst
beyond	bynd
big	bg
body	bdy
branch	brnch
break	brk
breakdown	brkdwn
bring	brng
bringing	brngng
bill	bl
billed	bld'
billing	blg
build	bld
builder	bldr
building	bldg
busy	bzy
business	bznz
but	bt
buy	by
buyer	byr
buying	byg

C

cash	csh
charge	chrj
chair	chr
chairman	chrmn
call	cl
calling	clg
caller	clr
can	cn
cannot	cnt
cancel	cnsl
cancelling	cnslg
cancelled	cnsld
change	chnj
chance	chnz
charge	chrj
check	chk
cheque	chq
claim	clm
come	cm
coming	cmg

contract	**cntrct**	dozen	**dzn**	form	**fm**
copy	**cpy**			formal	**fml**
cost	**cst**	**E**		from	**frm**
country	**cntry**	enclose	**nclz**	forgive	**fgv**
cover	**cvr**	enclosure	**nclzr**	forgiving	**fgvg**
credit	**crdt**	enclosing	**nclzg**	force	**fz**
current	**crnt**	enforce	**nfz**	forcing	**fzg**
currency	**crnzy**	enforcing	**nfzg**	forthcoming	**fthcmg**
		enforcement	**nfzm**	freehold	**frhld**
D		engage	**ngj**	furnish	**frnsh**
day	**dy**	engagement	**ngjmnt**	furnishing	**frnshg**
daily	**dyly**	enjoy	**njy**	furnisher	**frnshr**
date	**dt**	enjoying	**njyg**	further	**frthr**
debit	**dbt**	enjoyment	**njym**		
depart	**dprt**	enquire	**nqr**	**G**	
deposit	**dpzt**	enquiring	**nqrng**	garment	**grmnt**
develop	**dvlp**	enquiry	**nqry**	give	**gv**
development	**dvlpm**	example	**xmpl**	giving	**gvg**
detail	**dtl**	exam	**xm**	gone	**gn**
did	**dd**	examine	**xmn**	going	**gwng**
difficult	**dfclt**	examining	**xmng**	government	**gvmnt**
direct	**drct**	export	**xpt**	governmental	**gvmntl**
director	**drctr**			grateful	**grtfl**
directing	**drctg**	**F**		grant	**grnt**
discharge	**dschrj**	face	**fs**	guaranty	**grnty**
dissatisfied	**dstsfd**	facing	**fsg**	guarantied	**grntyd**
dissatisfaction	**dstsfcn**	fact	**fct**	guaranteeing	**grntyg**
distance	**dstnz**	factory	**fctry**		
despatch	**dspch**	family	**fmly**	**H**	
discover	**dscvr**	fashion	**fshn**	had	**hd**
discovery	**dscvry**	fashionable	**fshnbl**	half	**hf**
discovering	**dscvrng**	fasten	**fsn**	hand	**hnd**
document	**dcmnt**	favour	**fvr**	handed	**hndd**
documentary	**dcmntry**	favourable	**fvrbl**	handing	**hndg**
documentation		firm	**fhm**	handle	**hndl**
	dcmntzn	figure	**fgr**	handling	**hndlg**
does	**ds**	final	**fnl**	happen	**hpn**
down	**dwn**	finality	**fnlty**	happening	**hpng**
draft	**drft**	find	**fnd**	happy	**hpy**
direction	**drcn**	fast	**fst**	hardware	**hrdwr**
doing	**dwng**	first	**frst**	hardship	**hrdshp**
done	**dn**	for	**f**	has	**hz**

have	**hv**	joining	**jng**	method	**mthd**
having	**hvg**	just	**jst**	middle	**mdl**
hang	**hng**			miss	**ms**
hanging	**hngng**	**K**		mrs	**mrs**
he	**h**	kept	**kpt**	month	**mnth**
help	**hlp**	kind	**knd**	monthly	**mnthly**
helping	**hlpg**	kindly	**kndly**	must	**mst**
helped	**hlpd**			move	**mv**
hereby	**hrby**	**L**		moving	**mvg**
herein	**hrn**	labour	**lbr**	much	**mch**
herewith	**hwth**	large	**lrj**		
him	**hm**	largely	**lrjly**	**N**	
himself	**hmslf**	last	**lzt**	name	**nm**
her	**hr**	leaflet	**lflt**	named	**nmd**
herself	**hrslf**	left	**lft**	naming	**nmg**
his	**hs**	less	**ls**	namely	**nmly**
him	**hm**	local	**lcl**	near	**nr**
himself	**hmslf**	locality	**lclty**	nearing	**nrng**
hotel	**htl**	long	**lng**	nearly	**nrly**
how	**hw**	longterm	**lngtrm**	news	**nwz**
however	**hwvr**	low	**lw**	newspaper	**nwzppr**
		lower	**lwr**	next	**nxt**
I		lowering	**lwrg**	nothing	**nthg**
import	**mpt**			not	**nt**
important	**mptnt**	**M**		noting	**ntg**
importance	**mptnz**	make	**mk**	notation	**ntzn**
impossible	**mpsbl**	making	**mkg**	nothing	**nthg**
impossibility	**mpsblty**	made	**md**	now	**nw**
in	**n**	magazine	**mgzn**	number	**nmbr**
indirect	**ndrct**	manufacture	**mnfctr**	numbering	**nmbrng**
indirectly	**ndrctly**	manufacturing	**mnfctrg**		
industry	**ndstry**	manufacturer	**mnfr**	**O**	
industrial	**ndstryl**	margin	**mrjn**	of	**v**
inside	**nsd**	mark	**mrk**		
insure	**nzr**	market	**mrkt**	**P**	
insurance	**nzrnz**	marketing	**mrktg**	pack	**pk**
invoice	**nvz**	may	**my**	packing	**pkg**
invoicing	**nvzg**	maybe	**myb**	pamphlet	**pmflt**
is	**s**	medical	**mdcl**	part	**prt**
		medicine	**mdzn**	partner	**prtnr**
J		message	**mzj**	partnership	**prtnrshp**
join	**jn**	messenger	**mznjr**	pass	**ps**

passport	**pspt**	repayment	**rpmnt**	should	**shd**
pay	**py**	repaying	**rpyg**	share	**shr**
paying	**pyg**	reward	**rwrd**	shareholder	**shrhldr**
payment	**pmnt**	rewarded	**rwrdd**	small	**sml**
perhaps	**prhps**	rewarding	**rwrdg**	smaller	**smlr**
period	**prd**	rise	**rz**	some	**sm**
person	**prsn**	rising	**rzg**	something	**smthng**
personal	**prsnl**	risen	**rzn**	someone	**smwn**
pleasure	**plzr**	room	**rm**	somewhere	**smwhr**
pleasant	**plznt**			side	**sd**
prepare	**prpr**	**S**		show	**shw**
price	**prc**	sale	**zl**	showing	**shwng**
public	**pblc**	salesman	**zlsmn**	ship	**shp**
publication	**pblczn**	saleswoman	**zlswmn**	shipment	**shpm**
publish	**pblsh**	salesmanship	**zlsmnshp**	shipping	**shpg**
publisher	**pblshr**	sample	**smpl**	some	**sm**
purchase	**prchz**	satisfied	**stsfd**	someone	**smwn**
purchaser	**prchzr**	satisfaction	**stsfcn**	soon	**sn**
position	**pzn**	satisfactory	**stsfctry**	sorry	**sry**
post	**pst**	satisfactorily	**stsfctrly**	stand	**stnd**
posting	**pstg**	save	**sv**	standing	**stndg**
postpone	**pstpn**	saving	**svg**	stay	**sty**
postponement	**pstpnm**	saw	**zw**	stayed	**styd**
		say	**zy**	staying	**styg**
Q		saying	**zyg**	still	**stl**
quick	**qk**	say	**sy**	supply	**sply**
quickly	**qkly**	saying	**syg**	supplying	**splyg**
		said	**zd**	supplier	**splyr**
R		sell	**sl**	sure	**zr**
range	**rnj**	seller	**slg**		
ranges	**rnjs**	seller	**slr**	**T**	
record	**rcd**	self	**slf**	take	**tk**
regard	**rgd**	selves	**slvs**	taking	**tkg**
regarding	**rgdg**	session	**zsn**	taken	**tkn**
remark	**rmrk**	second	**scnd**	table	**tbl**
remarking	**rmrkg**	secondary	**scndry**	thank	**tnk**
remarkable	**rmrkbl**	secondhand	**scndhnd**	thanked	**tnkd**
remove	**rmv**	set	**zt**	thanking	**tnkg**
removing	**rmvg**	settle	**ztl**	thankful	**tnkfl**
removal	**rmvl**	settling	**ztlg**	the	**th**
removable	**rmvbl**	settlement	**ztlmnt**	they	**thy**
repay	**rpy**	shall	**shl**	their	**thyr**

there	**thr**	with	**wth**
therefore	**thrfr**	withstand	**wthstnd**
therein	**thrn**	wonder	**wndr**
these	**thz**	wondering	**wndrg**
to	**t**	world	**wrld**
together	**tgthr**	worldwide	**wrldwyd**
toward	**twrd**	would	**wd**
today	**tdy**	work	**wrk**
trade	**trd**	worker	**wrkr**
trader	**trdr**	working	**wrkg**
trademark	**trdmrk**	worker	**wrkr**
travel	**trvl**	workable	**wrkbl**
traveller	**trvlr**	write	**wrt**
travelling	**trvlg**	writing	**wrtg**
telephone	**tlfn**	written	**wrtn**

V

very	**vry**

W

wage	**wj**
wait	**wt**
waiting	**wtg**
walk	**wlk**
walking	**wlkg**
warehouse	**wrhwz**
was	**wz**
water	**wtr**
way	**wy**
were	**wr**
welcome	**wlcm**
welcoming	**wlcmg**
what	**wht**
wholesale	**whlzl**
wholesaler	**whlzlr**
will	**wl**
wish	**wsh**
wishing	**wshg**
when	**whn**
where	**whr**
whether	**wthr**
which	**wch**

Y

yard	**yrd**
yesterday	**ystrdy**
yet	**yt**
your	**y**
yourself	**yslf**
yourselves	**yslvs**
young	**yng**
youngster	**yngstr**

AgiliWriting

THE READABLE SHORTHAND
OF THE ENGLISH LANGUAGE

HARE-RAISERS

AgiliWriting shorthand practice from dictation
by the author. *(Includes two tapes)*

ISTS

DICTIONARY OF STRINGS

mn	above mentioned	**aztcnt**	as it cannot
nmd	above named	**aztcntb**	as it cannot be
zu	advise you	**aslngs**	as long as
tm	all the time	**aslngspsb**	as long as possible
cn	all we can	**aslngswcn**	as long as we can
y	any day	**aslngsucn**	as long as you can
ynw	any day now	**asmchs**	as much as
cnv	any inconvenience	**asmchspsb**	as much as possible
nvdy	any time of day	**asprtlcn**	as per telephone conversation
n	any time	**asprurtlcn**	as per our telephone conversation
x	approximately		
'xmz	a very merry Xmas	**aspsb**	as possible
'xmz'	a very merry Christmas	**asrq**	as requested
s	as far as	**asrqbu**	as requested by you
sino	as far as I know	**asrqnmylv**	as requested in my letter of
spsb	as far as possible		
swno	as far as we know	**asrqnylv**	as requested in your letter of
ws	as follows		
znt	as it does not	**asns**	as soon as
nt	as it is not	**asnsicn**	as soon as I can
vznt	as it was not	**asnspsb**	as soon as possible
vdnt	as it would not	**asap**	as soon as possible
vdntb	as it would not be	**asnsthyrbl**	as soon as they are able

asnsthycn	as soon as they can
asnswrbl	as soon as we are able
asnswcn	as soon as we can
asnsIno	as soon as I know
asnsthyno	as soon as they know
asnswno	as soon as we know
asnsucn	as soon as you can
asnsthycn	as soon as they can
aswcnt	as we cannot
aswno	as we know
aswls	as well as
asuno	as you know
azruvrbstn	assure you of our best attention
azrngu	assuring you
azrnguvrbstn	assuring you of our best attention
atl	at all
atlpsb	at all possible
atltms	at all times
atnywntm	at any one time
atnytm	at any time
atwnz	at once
athbstvtms	at the best of times
athmom	at the moment
athprztm	at the present time
athrqv	at the request of
athzmtm	at the same time
athtmv	at the time of
athtmvdy	at the time of day
athmom	at the moment
atyerlcnv	at your earliest convenience
atyverlcnv	at your very earliest convenience
b'drft	banker's draft
bdnbrd	bed and board
bdnbrk	bed and breakfast
bsrgds	best regards
bswshs	best wishes
b'o'l	bill of lading
bynby	by and by

bfcp	by first class post
bscp	by second class post
brp	by return post
brtlx	by return telex
bu	by you
cnb	can be
cnu	can you
cnub	can you
cnupls	can you please
cnuplcnf	can you please confirm
cnupldvthgpsb	can you please do everything possible
cnupldvthgucn	can you please do everything you can
cnuplfwd	can you please forward
cnuplfwdtus	can you please forward to us
cnupltusno	can you please let us know
cnupltmno	can you please let me know
cnuplsndus	can you please send us
cntb	cannot be
ctlgnpcl	catalogue and price list
srcs'	circulars
srcms	circumstances
clmfm	claim form
co's	company's
cnv	convenient
cnvn	convenience
cnvtmndt	convenient time and date
cdb	could be
cdntb	could not be
cdu	could you
cdupltusno	could you please let us know
cduplsndus	could you please send us
crntpcl	current price list
dtntm	date and time
d'o'b	date of birth
dybdy	day by day

dytdy	day to day	**folytlcl**	following your telephone call
d'gm	Dear Gentlemen		
dsr	Dear Sir	**folurtlcl**	following our telephone call
dsrs	Dear Sirs		
d's'm	Dear Sir/Madam	**fbhfv**	for and on behalf of
dlvdt	delivery date	**fnyncnv**	for any inconvenience
dlvns	delivery instructions	**fnyncnvczd**	for any inconvenience caused
dpt	department		
ddso	did so	**fnynfo**	for any information
ddthy	did they	**ftnv**	for attention of
ddthyno	did they know	**fthtnv**	for the attention of
ddthyhv	did they have	**fthfrstm**	for the first time
ddu	did you	**fthlstm**	for the last time
dduhv	did you have	**fthflwg**	for the following
dnt	do not	**fy**	for your
dso	do so	**fytn**	for your attention
du	do you	**fytnthsmtr**	for your attention to this matter
duno	do you know		
dc'crdt	documentary credit	**fycnv**	for your convenience
drngthwkcm	during the week commencing	**fynfo**	for your information
		frmdytdy	from day to day
erlcnv	earliest convenience	**frmtmtm**	from time to time
erlrp	early reply	**frmwktwk**	from week to week
eh	enclose herewith	**frmu**	from you
ehplfnd	enclosed herewith please find	**fulprtcs**	full particulars
		f'f'f	furniture fixtures and fittings
epf	enclosed please find	**frthnfo**	further information
evthgpsb	everything possible	**ftmlv**	further to my letter of
eda	expected date of arrival	**ftylv**	further to your letter of
eta	expected time of arrival	**ftrlv**	further to our letter of
fvrvyerlrp	favour of your early reply	**ftrqt**	further to our quotation of
		ftyqtv	further to your quotation of
fwdys	few days	**ftrtlclv**	further to our telephone call of
f'c	first class		
f'c'p	first class post	**ftrtlcnv**	further to our telephone conversation
fdv	first day of		
fdvthmnth	first day of the month	**ftrtlxv**	further to our telex of
fxftgs	fixtures and fittings	**ftytlxv**	further to your telex of
f'f	fixtures and fittings	**gvus**	give us
folnfo	following information	**gvu**	give you
folurtlcn	following our telephone conversation	**gvgus**	giving us
		gvgu	giving you

hdnt	had not
h'xmz	happy Xmas
h'xmz'	happy Christmas
h'p'ny	happy and prosperous New year
hzbn	has been
hznt	has not
hzntbn	has not been
hzntbnpsb	has not been possible
hvbn	have been
hvbnsntu	have been sent to you
hvu	have you
hvubn	have you been
hvubnabl	have you been able
hvuhd	have you had
hvnt	have not
hwlb	he will be
hlpu	help you
h'p	hire purchase
imdglicn	I am doing all I can
imehfytn	I am enclosing herewith for your attention
imgvgu	I am giving you
imv	I am of
implsd	I am pleased
Imvplsd	I am very pleased
implteh	I am pleased to enclose herewith
impltnfmu	I am pleased to inform you
imsry	I am sorry
imvsry	I am very sorry
imsrytnfmu	I am sorry to inform you
imvsrytnfmu	I am very sorry to inform you
imunbl	I am unable
imvpltnfmu	I am very pleased to inform you
icngvu	I can give you
icntgvu	I cannot give you
iddnt	I did not
iddntno	I did not know
ieh	I enclose herewith
iehfytn	I enclose herewith for your attention
ihv	I have
ihvbn	I have been
ihvhd	I have had
ihvntbn	I have not been
ihvntbnabl	I have not been able
ihvnthd	I have not had
ihvsntu'bfcp	I have sent you by first class post
ihvsntu'usc	I have sent you under separate cover
ihvwrtn	I have written
ino	I know
ilkfwd	I look forward
ilkfwdtzgu	I look forward to seeing you
imyb	I may be
imybabl	I may be able
imyhv	I may have
imyntb	I may not be
imyntbabl	I may not be able
imzb	I must be
imzntb	I must not be
nnsrtylv	in answer to your letter of
nacdwyrq	in accordance with your request
nacdwylv	in accordance with your letter of
nnycs	in any case
nmylv	in my letter of
nrptylv	in reply to your letter of
nyl	in your letter
nylv	in your letter of
irfrtmordr	I refer to my order
irftmono	I refer to my order no
irftyono	I refer to your order number
irftylv	I refer to your letter of
irgrt	I regret

irgrtnfmu	I regret to inform you
irqr	I require
ishlb	I shall be
Ishlbabl	I shall be able
Ishlbunbl	I shall be unable
ishdb	I should be
ishdnt	I should not
ishdntb	I should not be
iwz	I was
Iwznt	I was not
iwl	I will
iwlb	I will be
iwlbabl	I will be able
iwlbabltzu	I will be able to see you
iwlbpltltuhv	I will be pleased to let you have
iwlbunbl	I will be unable
Iwlbunbltzu	I will be unable to see you
iwldvthgpsb	I will do everything possible
iwlgvu	I will give you
iwlhv	I will have
iwlno	I will know
iwltuhv	I will let you have
iwltuno	I will let you know
iwlntbabl	I will not be able
iwlnthv	I will not have
iwlntrqr	I will not require
iwlrqr	I will require
iwshtnku	I wish to thank you
iwd	I would
iwdb	I would be
iwdbabl	I would be able
iwdlktzu	I would like to see you
iwdnt	I would not
iwdntb	I would not be
iwdntbabl	I would not be able
ifimabl	if I am able
iftcnb	if it can be
ifcntb	if it cannot be
iftzatlpsb	if it is at all possible

iftzpsb	if it is possible
iftwlbatlpsb	if it will be at all possible
iftwlbcnv	if it will be convenient
iftwlbpsb	if it will be possible
ifthrabl	if they are able
ifthrunbl	if they are unable
ifthycn	if they can
ifthycnb	if they can be
ifthycnt	if they cannot
ifthycd	if they could
ifthywlb	if they will be
ifwrabl	if we are able
ifwrunbl	if we are unable
ifwcn	ifwcn
ifwcnb	if we can be
ifwcnbvny	if we can be of any
ifwcnbvnyast	if we can be of any assistance
ifwcd	if we could
ifyrabl	if you are able
ifyrunbl	if you are unable
ifucn	if you can
ifucnb	if you can be
ifucndoso	if you can do so
ifucnt	if you cannot
ifucd	if you could
ifucdltmno	if you could let me now
ifucdlthmno	if you could let them know
ifucdltushv	if you could let us have
ifucdltusno	if you could let us know
ifucdpltusno	if you could please let us know
ifuwl	if you will
ifuwlb	if you will be
ifuwlbabl	if you will be able
ifuwd	if you would
ifuwdb	if you would be
ifuwdltmno	if you would let me know

ifuwdltusno	if you would let us know
imdatn	immediate attention
imdlvry	immediate delivery
nacdwy	in accordance with your
nacdwynq v	in accordance with your enquiry of
nacdwynstrcs	in accordance with your instructions
nacdwylv	in accordance with your letter of
nacdwyrq	in accordance with your request
nacdwyrqv	in accordance with your request of
nnsrtynqv	in answer to your enquiry of
nnsrtylv	in answer to your letter of
nnsrng	in answering
nnycs	in any case
nnywy	in any way
nasmch	in as much
ncsv	in case of
nthcsv	in the case of
ndwcs	in due course
nnclzg	in enclosing
nfvrv	in favour of
nfrntv	in front of
ngdtm	in good time
nlwv	in lieu of
nlnwth	in line with
nur	in our
nrlv	in our letter of
nropn	in our opinionm
nrptycblv	in reply to your cable of
nrptynqv	in reply to your enquiry of
nyl	in your letter
nrptylv	in reply to your letter of
nrptyqtv	in reply to your quotation of
nrptytlxv	in reply to your telex of
nsofrs	in so far as
nthcsv	in the case of
nthsrcms	in the circumstances
nthvntv	in the event of
nthfsv	in the face of
nthmntm	in the meantime
nthopnv	in the opinion of
nthsmv	in the sum of
nthrlv	in their letter of
nthzsrcms	in these circumstances
nthscs	in this case
nthscncn	in this connection
nthsmtr	in this matter
ntm	in time
nvwv	in view of
nyl	in your letter
nylv	in your letter of
nfmus	inform us
nfo	information
ir'l'c	irrevocable letter of credit
ztatlpsb	is it at all possible
ztpsb	is it possible
itcnb	it can be
itcntb	it cannot be
ithzbn	it has been
ithzntbn	it has not been
itz	it is
itzgngtb	it is going to be
itznt	it is not
itzntatlpsb	it is not at all possible
itzntgngtb	it is not going to be
itzntgngtb'	it isn't going to be
itzntpsb	it is not possible
itzntpsb'	it isn't possible
itzv	it is of
itzuropn	it is our opinion
itshlb	it shall be
itwz	it was
itwznt	it was not
itwl	it will
itwlb	it will be
itwlbcnv	it will be convenient

itwlntbcnv	it will not be convenient
itwlbpsb	it will be possible
itwlntbpsb	it will not be possible
itwlbsntu	it will be sent to you
itwlntb	it will not be
itwd	it would
itwdb	it would be
itwdbpsb	it would be possible
itwdnt	it would not
itwdnt'	it wouldn't
itwdntb	it would not be
itwdntb'	it wouldn't be
itwdntbpsb	it would not be possible
itwdntbpsb'	it wouldn't be possible
kndrgds	kind regards
lstdyv	last day of
lzdyvthmnth	last day of the month
lstm	last time
lstwk	lztwk
lstyr	last year
lstyrs	last year's
lsnls	less and less
ltmno	let me know
lthmno	let him no
ltus	let us
ltushv	let us have
ltusno	let us know
l'c	letter of credit
mntnks	many thanks
mntnksfylv	many thanks for your letter of
mtrvfct	matter of fact
myb	may be
mybabl	may be able
myntb	may not be
myntbabl	may not be able
mybunbl	may be unable
mywbrngtytn	may we bring to your attention
m'a'a	Memorandum & Articles of Association
mornmor	more and more
mzb	must be
mzntb	must not be
mylv	my letter of
myrq	my request
nmadrztlno	name address and telephone no
nmnadrz	name and address
nmsnadrzs	name and addresses
nxfwdys	next few days
nxfwmnths	next few months
nxfwks	next few weeks
nxmnth	next month
nxmnths'	next month's
nxtm	next time
nxwks'	next week's
nnovr	none of our
nnvthtm	none of the time
ntb	not be
ovrbstn	of our best attention
ovrbstnatltms	of our best attention at all times
onbhfv	on behalf of
onur	on our
onthqstnv	on the question of on you
onybhf	on your behalf
wnznfal	once and for all
urlv	our letter of
urono	our order no
ono	order no
otvdt	out of date
otvdrs	out of doors
o's	outstanding
prtcs	particulars
plakrv	please acknowledge receipt of
pladvus	please advise us
plscnfm	please confirm
pldvthgucn	please do everything you can
plfndeh	please find enclosed herewith

plgvus	please give us
plfwd	please forward
plfwdasap	please forward as soon as possible
plnfmus	please inform us
pltmhv	please let me have
pltushv	please let us have
pltusno	please let us know
plsndus	please send us
plsndusasap	please send us as soon as possible
plsgnnzl	please sign and seal
plwdudso	please would you do so
pstdtd	postdated
pcl	price list
p'c	private & confidential
profma	pro forma
prods	products
rytlcl	re your telephone call
ryono	re your order no
rvyono	receipt of your order no
rvyqtv	receipt of your quotation of
rqbu	request by you
rop'	return of post
rtp	return post
rndnabt	round and about
smtm	some time
zmtm	same time
s'c	second class
s'c'p	second class post
zu	see you
zgu	seeing you
sae'	stamped addressed envelope
slfxpln	self explanatory
sndus	send us
sndu	send you
sndgu	sending you
sndgtu	sending to you
shwlb	she will be
shdb	should be
shdhvbn	should have been
shdnthvbn	should not have been
shdu	should you
snzrapls	sincere apologies
sofr	so far
sofrs	so far as
sofrswcn	so far as we can
sofrswno	so far as we know
s'p'c	strictly private & confidential
lcl	telephone call
tlclv	telephone call of
tlcn	telephone conversation
tlcnv	telephone conversation
tlcnv'	telephone conversation of
tlno	telephone number
tlu	tell you
trmsncnds	terms and conditions
t'o's	terms of sale
tnku	thank you
tufynqv	thank you for your enquiry of
tufylv	thank you for your letter of
tnkgu	thanking you
thtwz	that was
thtwcn	that we can
thtwhvbn	that we have been
thtwhvbnabl	that we have been able
thtwhvbnunbl	that we have been unable
thbvmn	the above mentioned
thbvmnsbj	the above mentioned subject
thbstm	the best time
thfolnfo	the following information
thnxfwdys	the next few days
thrwlb	there will be
thrwlntb	there will not be
thrabl	they are able
thrunbl	they are unable
thrdglthycn	they are doing all they can
thrdgvthgpsb	they are doing everything possible

thrgng	they are going
thrntgng	they are not going
thrvthopn	they are of the opinion
thyddnt	they did not
thydd	they did
thyddntno	they did not know
thyhv	they have
thyhvbn	they have been
thyhvntbn	they have not been
thyhvntbn'	they haven't been
thyhvbnabl	they have been able
thyhvbnunbl	they have been unable
thyhvntbnabl'	they haven't been able
thyhvcnf	they have confirmed
thyhvhd	they have had
thyhvnt	they have not
thyhvnt'	they haven't
thyhvntbnabl	they have not been able
thyhvnthd	they have not had
thyhvnthd'	they haven't had
thyno	they know
thydntno	they do not know
thylkfwdtzgu	they look forward to seeing you
thymyb	they may be
thymybabl	they may be able
thymyntb	they may not be
thymyntbabl	they may not be able
thymzb	they must be
thymzntb	they must not be
thyrqr	they require
thyshd	they should
thyshdb	they should be
thyshdbabl	they should be able
thyshdhv	they should have
thyshdntb	they should not be
thyshdnthv	they should not have
thywr	they were
thywrabl	they were able
thywrnt	they were not
thywrntabl	they were not able
thywrunbl	they were unable
thywlb	they will be
thywlbgng	they will be going
thywlclus	they will call us
thywldlthycn	they will do all they can
thywldvthgpsb	they will do everything possible
thywldwhthycn	they will do what they can
thywlhv	they will have
thywltmhv	they will let me have
thywltmno	they will let me know
thywltushv	they willlet us have
thywltusno	they will let us know
thywlntb	they will not be
thywlntbabl	they will not be able
thywlnthv	they will not have
thywlntrqr	they will not require
thywlrqr	they will require
thywd	they would
thywdb	they would be
thywdbabl	they would be able
thywdlktno	they would like to know
thywdlktzu	they would like to see you
thywdnt	they would not
thywdntb	they would not be
thywdntb'	they wouldn't be
thywdntbabl	they would not be able
thywdntbabl'	they wouldn't be able
thywdntrqr	they would not require
thywdntrqr'	they wouldn't require
thsmtr	this matter
thswz	this was
thswk	this week
thsyr	this year
thyrs'	this year's

tmvdy	time of day
tb	to be
tdt	to date
tdysdt	today's date
tdso	to do so
tgvu	to give you
tnfmu	to inform you
tltuno	to let you know
tur	to our
tzu	to see you
ttlu	to tell you
tus	to us
tu	to you
tytn	to your attention
tylv	to your letter of
undnvno	under invoice no
usc	under separate cover
uptdt	up to date
uptdtnfo	up to date information
uptdtpzn	up to date position
updtd	updated
upnu	upon you
urjatnthsmtr	urgent attention to this matter
vbswshs	very best wishes
wznt	was not
w	w
wak	we acknowledge
wakrv	we acknowledge receipt of
wakrvyqtv	we acknowledge receipt of your quotation of
wakrvrnqv	we acknowledge receipt of your enquiry of
wakrvylv	we acknowledge receipt of your letter of
wakrvyordv	we acknowledge receipt of your order of
wakrvyono	we acknowledge receipt of your order no
wakrvyord	we acknowledge receipt of your order

wakrvyordv	we acknowledge receipt of your order of
wakrvytlxv	we acknowledge receipt of your telex of
wakwtnks	we acknowledge with thanks
wapljz	we apologise
waplfnyncnv	we apologise for any inconvenience
wrabl	we are able
wrawtg	we are awaiting
wrunbl	we are unable
wrdwng	we are doing
wrdglwcn	we are doing all we can
wrdgvthgpsb	we are doing everything possible
wrdgvthgwcn	we are doing everything we can
wrdgrbst	we are doing our best
wreh	we are enclosing herewith
wrehfytn	we are enclosing herewith for your attention
wrfwdgfytn	we are forwarding for your attention
wrfwdg	we are forwarding
wrfwdgtusc	we are forwarding to you under separate cover
wrnfvrv	we are in favour of
wrnrv	we are in receipt of
wrnrvycblv	we are in receipt of your cable of
wrnrvynqv	we are in receipt of your enquiry of
wrnrvylv	we are in receipt of your letter of
wrnrvyqtv	we are in receipt of your quotation of
wrnrvytlxv	we are in receipt of your telex of
wrv	we are of
wrvcs	we are of course

wrdglwcn	we are doing all we can	**wrwrtgtltuno**	we are writing to let you know
wrotvstk	we are out of stock	**wrwrtgttlu**	we are writing to tell you
wrpltqt	we are pleased to quote	**wrwrtgtnku**	we are writing to thank you
wrpltqtu	we are pleased to quote you	**wazru**	we assure you
wrpl	we are pleased	**wawt**	we await
wrpltadvzu	we are pleased to advise you	**wawtynstrcs**	we await your instructions
wrplteh	we are pleased to enclose herewith	**wawtyfrthnstrcs**	we await your further instructions
wrpltehfytn	we are pleased to enclose herewith for your attention	**wawtyerladvz**	we await your early advice
wrpltnfmu	we are pleased to inform you	**wawtyerlrpl**	we await your early reply
wrpltltuno	we are pleased to let you know	**wawtyrpl**	we await your reply
wrpltqtzflws	we are pleased to quote as follows:-	**wawtyrplbrp**	we await your reply by return post
wrsndgu	we are sending you	**wcn**	we can
wrsndguh	we are sending you herewith	**wcnazru**	we can assure you
wrsndgusc	we are sending you under separate cover	**wcnb**	we can be
wrsry	we are sorry	**wcntb**	we cannot be
wrvsry	we are very sorry	**wcnt'**	we can't
wrsrytnfmu	we are sorry to inform you	**wcnb'**	we can't be
wrvsrytnfmu	we are very sorry to inform you	**wcnfrvyono**	we confirm receipt of your order no
wrsryttlu	we are sorry to tell you	**wcnfrv**	we confirm receipt of
wrzr	we are sure	**wcnfrvylv**	we confirm receipt of your letter of
wrvpltnfmu	we are very pleased to inform you	**wcnfrvyordv**	we confirm receipt of your order of
wrwtg	we are waiting	**wcnfrvyqtv**	we confirm receipt of your quotation of
wrwlgnabl	we are willing and able	**wcnfrvytlxv**	we confirm receipt of your telex of
wrwrtg	we are writing	**wcdb**	we could be
wrwrtgtadvzu	we are writing to advise you	**wcdntb**	we could not be
wrwrtgtnfmu	we are writing to inform you	**wcdntb'**	we couldn't be
		wdd	we did
		wddnt	we did not
		wddnt'	we didn't

wddntno	we did not know
wddntno'	we didn't know
wdnt	we do not
wdntno	we do not know
wnclz	we enclose
weh	we enclose herewith
wehfytn	we enclose herewith for your attention
wesae	we enclose stamped addressed envelope
wesaefyrp	we enclose stamped addressed envelope for your reply
whv	we have
whvhd	we have had
whvnthd	we have not had
whvbn	we have been
whvbnabl	we have been able
whvntbnabl	we have not been able
whvbnunbl	we have been unable
whvdnlwcn	we have done all we can
whvdnvthgpsb	we have done everything possible
whvdnrbst	we have done our best
whvfwdd	we have forwarded
whvfwddtu	we have forwarded to you
whvfwddtusc	we have forwarded to you under separate cover
whvhd	we have had
whvnt	we have not
whvnt'	we haven't
whvntbn	we have not been
whvntbn'	we haven't been
whvntbnabl	we have not been able
whvntbnabl'	we haven't been able
whvnthd	we have not had
whvnthd'	we haven't had
whvplznfmgu	we have pleasure in informing you

whvrylv	we have received your letter of
whvrq	we have requested
whvsntusc	we have sent you under separate cover
whvsntu	we have sent you
whvwrtn	we have written
whvntny	we haven't any
whvntnymor	we haven't any more
wno	we know
wnov	we know of
wnovnorsnwy	we know of no reason why
wlkfwd	we look forward
wlkfwdtzgu	we look forward to seeing you
wmy	we may
wmyb	we may be
wmybabl	we may be able
wmyhv	we may have
wmyntb	we may not be
wmyntbabl	we may not be able
wmz	we must
wmzb	we must be
wmznfmu	we must inform you
wmzntb	we must not be
wmzy	we must say
wrfr	we refer
wrfrturlv	we refer to our letter of
wrfrtono	we refer to our order no
wrfrtyono	we refer to your order no
wrfrthbvmn	we refer to the above mentioned
wrfrthbvono	we refer to the above order no
wrfrtybvono	we refer to your above order no
wrfrtynqv	we refer to your enquiry of
wrfrtylv	we refer to your letter of

wrfrtyqtv	we refer to your quotation of
wrfrtytlfncl	we refer to your telephone call
wrfru	we refer you
wrgrt	we regret
wrgrtadvzu	we regret to advise you
wrgrtnfmu	we regret to inform you
wrmhn	we remain
wrqstd	we requested
wrqstg	we are requesting
wshlb	we shall be
wshlbpl	we shall be pleased
wshlbvpl	we shall be very pleased
wshlvcs	we shall of course
wshd	we should
wshdb	we should be
wshdbabl	we should be able
wshdhv	we should have
wshdnt	we should not
wsnzrgrt	we sincerely regret
wsnzrgrtadvzu	we sincerely regret to advise you
wtnku	we thank you
wtu	we thank you
wtufynqv	we thank you for your enquiry of
wtufyqtv	we thank you for your quotation of
wtufykndtn	we thank you for your kind attention
wtufylv	we thank you for your letter of
wtufyono	we thank you for your order no
wtufyordv	we thank you for your order of
wtufytlxv	we thank you for your telex of
wwr	we were
wwrabl	we were able
wwrunbl	we were unable
wwrntabl	we were not able
wwrpltrzv	we were pleased to receive
wwrvpltrzv	we were very pleased to receive
wwrsry	we were sorry
wwrvsry	we were very sorry
wwl	we will
wwlb	we will be
wwlbabl	we will be able
wwlntbabl	we will not be able
wwlbunbl	we will be unable
wwlclu	we will call you
wwlbclgu	we will be calling you
wwlbfwdg	we will be forwarding
wwlbfwdgtu	we will be forwarding to you
wwlbfwdgtusc	we will be forwarding to you under separate cover
wwlbpltzu	we will be pleased to see you
wwlbpltsndu	we will be pleased to send you
wwldo	we will do
wwldvthgwcn	we will do everything we can
wwldlwcn	we will do all we can
wwldvthgpsb	we will do everything possible
wwldrbst	we will do our best
wwlfwd	we will forward
wwlfwdtu	we will forward to you
wwlbfwdgtu	we will be forwarding to you
wwlgvu	we will give you
wwlhv	we will have
wwlnfmu	we will inform you
wwlno	we will know
wwltuhv	we will let you have
wwltuno	we will let you know
wwlntb	we will not be

wwlntbabl	we will not be able
wwlnthv	we will not have
wwlrqr	we will require
wwlntrqr	we will not require
wwlnfmu	we will inform you
wwlntb	we will not be
wlntbabl	we will not be able
wwlvcrz	we will of course
wwlsndu	we will send you
wwsh	we wish
wwshtno	we wish to know
wwshu	we wish you
wwd	we would
wwdaprz	we would appreciate
wwdaprz	we would appreciate
wwdaprzyerlrp	we would appreciate your early reply
wwdb	we would be
wwdbabl	we would be able
wwdbpl	we would be pleased
wwdlktno	we would like to know
wwdlktzu	we would like to see you
wwdnt	we would not
wwdntb	we would not be
wwdntbabl	we would not be able
wwdrqr	we would require
wwdrqu	we would request you
wwrtltuno	we write to let you know
wktwk	week to week
wk's	week's
welnntus	well known to us
wrabl	we are able
wrunbl	we are unable
wrnt	were not
wncnu	when can you
wncnub	when can you be
wncnusndus	when can you send us
wnddthy	when did they
wnddu	when did you
wnwltbcnv	when will it be convenient

wnwltb	when will it be
wnwltbpsb	when will it be possible
wnwlu	when will you
wyddthy	why did they
wyddu	why did you
wyddnthy	why didn't they
whyhvu	why have you
wyhvnthy	why haven't they
wlb	will be
wldo	will do
wldso	will do so
wldvthgwcn	will do everything we can
wldvthgpsb	will do everything possible
wltbcnv	will it be convenient
wltuno	will let you know
wlu	will you
wlupltmno	will you please let me know
wlupltusno	will you please let us know
wluplsnd	will you please send
wluplsndus	will you please send us
wthlgdwshs	with all good wishes
wthbswhs	with best wishes
wthbsrgds	with best regards
wthknrgds	with kind regards
wrf	with reference
wrftmono	with reference to my order no
wrftyono	with reference to your order no
wrftono	with reference to our order no
wrftyabvono	with reference to your above order no
wrftylv	with reference to your letter of
wrfrtybvono	we refer to your above order no
wrfrtyono	we refer to your order no

wthu	with you
wthnxfwdys	within the next few days
wdb	would be
wwdb	we would be
wdbaprz	would be appreciated
wdbgrtaprz	would be greatly appreciated
wdntb	would not be
wdu	would you
wdupltusno	would you please let us know
wdtbpsb	would it be possible
wrgtnfmu	we regret to inform you
ydysdt	yesterday's date
yrabl	you are able
yrnt	you are not
yrntabl	you are not able
ucn	you can
ucnt	you cannot
uddntno	you did not know
uhv	you have
uhvhd	you have had
uhvnt	you have not
uhvnt'	you haven't
uno	you know
umyb	you may be
umybabl	you may be able
umyhv	you may have
umyrqr	you may require
umzb	you must be
ushd	you should
ushdb	you should be
ushdhv	you should have
ushdnt	you should not
ushdntb	you should not be
uwl	you will
uwlb	you will be
uwlbabl	you will be able
uwlbunbl	you will be unable
uwlntbabl	you will not be able
uwd	you would

uwdb	you would be
uwdbabl	you would be able
ytlxv	your telex of
ycblv	your cable of
ylv	your letter of
yerlcnv	your early convenience
yerltn	your early attention
yerlrp	your early reply
ynmndrz	your name and address
yono	your order no
yqtv	your quotation of
yrq	your request
yrqv	your request of
yrp	your reply
yrpbrp	your reply by return post
ysn	Yours sincerely
ytlcl	your telephone call
ytlclv	your telephone call of
yurjtn	your urgent attention
yurjtnthsmtr	your urgent attention to this matter
ylv	your letter of
y's	your's
yf	yours faithfully
ysn	yours sincerely
ytruly	yours truly
yvtruly	yours very truly
yf	Yours faithfully

Agili+Plus

ADVANCES THE PRINCIPLES
OF AGILIWRITING SHORTHAND

IT'S TWICE AS FAST!

Agili+Plus uses only the standard letters
of the English alphabet.

ANSWERS

Answers to Exercises: Chapter 2, HAVING A GO

ROOT WORDS:
Exercise 1.
   srvg, cnsrv, cnsrvg, dsrv, dsrvg, rsrv, rsrvg
Exercise 2.
   tndg, cntnd, cntndg, dstnd, dstndg, xtnd, xtndg, ntnd, ntndg
Exercise 3.
   votg, dvot, dvotg

DELETION OF THE VOWELS
Exercise 1.
   difr, filtr, shivr, batl, lamnt, dsmantl, bothr, dvot, dplomt, mony, rnovt,
   bunglw, puzl, rustc, multpl
Exercise 2.
   itm, idl, ablty, afnty, atnd, anx, ofr, oblgt, objctv, obstcl, opn, ordr, optmst,
   utlty, undr, undrstnd, utr.
Exercise 3.
   evad, erod, eratc, emotv, evolv, advoct, abortv, imobl, irvocbl, ignor,
   amortz.

REPEATED VOWELS:
Exercise 1.
btr, btwn, clvr, hrslf, ltr, lvl, nglctd, nvr, nvthls, prsnt, prtnd, prvnt, rlntd, rndr, rnw, rvlr, tlx, wstrn

Exercise 2.
svc, svl, svlty, crtc, clnc, dgnty, dmnsh, fnsh, mnstr, sgnfy, tmd, tmdty, vctm

Exercise 3.
cnl, cvlry, fntsy, hphzrd, hzrd, mdm, stndrd, vgrnt, vndl

Exercise 4.
efct, ejct, elct, erct, evnt, adpt, atch, atrct, awrd

THE VOWEL 'I'
Exercise 1.
britl, difr, fidl, filtr, hidn, litr, ridl, shivr, tipd, winr

Exercise 2.
byd, crym, dyn, dyv, dyvr, fyr, hyd, hyr, lyn. myn, ryfl, wyd, wydn, wyl

Exercise 3.
idl, idntfy, il, irspctv, itm

Exercise 4.
abyd, afyr, ignyt, unyt

Exercise 5.
bryt, fyt, gyd, hytn, ly, tyd, rplyd, tyt, tytn

Exercise 6.
alyd, aplyd

THE VOWEL 'U'
Exercise 1.
bufr, bundl, butr, dduct, fundmntl, rdundnt, sumr

Exercise 2.
bwgl, brwtl, cmwt, cmpwt, cmpwtr, rfwt, stwdnt, twtr

Exercise 3.
undr, undrstnd, upr, upwrd, unls, ultmt, unfy, utnsl, unt, unty, urbn, urbnty, utlty

Exercise 4.
acwt, astwt, imwn, imwtbl, obscwr, obscwrty

DIPTHONGS 1.
Exercise 1.
dvyt, dyry, dyt, mlyn, mtryl, mdyt, prmyt, provrbyl, rblyn, rlybl, thytr, scrtryl, vylnt
Exercise 2.
prvyz, rblyz, sryz
Exercise 3.
abrvyt, alvyt, imdyt, onyn, oryntl, ultryr, unyn, oblvyn, oblvyz

DIPTHONGS 2
Exercise 1.
crwlty, flwd, flwnt, fluctwtd, prptwl, pwtry, rwn, vrtwl, vrtwz
Exercise 2.
cntnwd, cntnwl, cntnwz, cnspcwz
Exercise 3.
aflwnt, anwl, acrwl, actwl, evlwt, evcwt, obtwry

LINKED VOWELS
Exercise 1.
bwlr, bwk, bwst, bwnd, bwndry, cwl, cwch, cwnt, cwntr, fwlt, flwndr, frwd, frwt, lwk, lwd, lwn, mwnt, pwnt, pwnd, prwd, rwnd, stwd, twst, twk, vwlt.
Exercise 2.
abwt, abrwd, abwnd, acwnt, alwd, amwnt, arwnd, astwnd, undrstwd
Exercise 3.
brawt, fawt, dawtr, dstrawt, hawty, nawty, slawtr, sawt, tawt.

SHORTS
Exercise 1.
cn, cm, crspnd, cstmr, dly, dy, dd, dn, frm, knd, gt, gn, hpy, hp, hr, hm, hmslf, hs, n, s, nn, psbl, sm, sn, vry, wy.
Exercise 2.
bnkg, cshg, crdtg, fndg, mrktg, mvg, prtg, rmvg, syg, tkg, wtg.
Exercise 3.
a) W hv bnkd th crdts snt tdy n th pst
b) Thy sy thy wl dlvr th wkly nws mgzn t m.
c) Th drctrs wl b mkg mny jrnys t Lndn ths yr
d) Th tw gsts wl lv th dbl rm n th htl bfr nxt Mndy
e) W r hpy t wrt tht w hv nw snt th chq t th cstmr n Wnchstr
f) w thnk tht th wkly rntl fgr s sn t b dbld.

Answers to Exercises: Chapter 17 SHORTS

1. W wl b zg thm vry sn.
2. H zd h wd wrt t m bfr th shw.
3. S thr ny wy w cn gt thyr csh bxs t thm tdy?
4. W zw ur frnds n Wnchstr ystrdy. Thy hv a vry bzy bznz thr.
5. Dd u snd thm th smpls thy rqstd?
6. Thy r lkly t b trvlg t Jpn n Sptmbr.
7. W hpg t mk th lng jrny t z ur frnds n th mnth v My.
8. Ur cstmrs wr vry plsd wth th gds w dlvrd t thm.
9. N wch cntry wl u b tkg y hldys ths yr?
10. Whn cn u gv m a brkdwn v th rtl fgrs t b gvn t th bnk.
11. W shd b grtfl if u cd nw ztl y bl.
12. Thr r sm vry chp gds t b hd n th mrkts.

The AGILIWRITING DICTIONARY contains approximately 11,000 short-hand abbreviations.

INDEX

Pr = Chapter on **Principles**.
QLG = **Quick learning Guide**.
HaG = **Having a Go**.

AgiliTyping ®

Software translates **AgiliWriting** shorthand into the full standard English language form.

AgiliTyping ®

Software for **COMPUTER USERS**

* Translates **AgiliWriting** shorthand into full standard English language form
* Runs on **IBM PC & compatibles**
* High speed operation
* Simple to use
* Operates with **Wordstar** or compatible software
* Built-in dictionary of approximately **8,000** words
* Dictionaries user extendible
* Available on **3.1/2** and **5.1/4 disks.**

Using **AgiliTyping**
Needs no special typing training.

Once the **AgiliWriting** shorthand text is typed into the computer and stored, the **AgiliTyping** software will read this in and translate it into full English language. When abbreviations are met which are not recognised, these are left untouched in the text. The expanded text can then be displayed, saved and printed out as with any word-processed text.

The **AgiliTyping** dictionary is user extendible and the fascination of constructing your own abbreviated writing, i.e. your own personal shorthand, for automatic transcription into full English language, is available to you with **AgiliTyping** software.

The Use of STRINGS
The ability to use **strings of words in ultra-shorthand forms** offers many labour saving and exciting possibilities for the user. These **STRINGS*** further abbreviate the basic shorthand by **stringing together words in commonly-used phrases** and thus, speed up the writing of the shorthand. The user can extend the dictionary of phrases by creating phrases of their own design. During the automatic transcription of this shorthand back into full English language, the software automatically re-creates the spaces between the words, for e.g.

Nrptylv 6 Sptmbr, wrpltnfmu thtwcn imdytly sply th cmpwtr u rqr. Pltusno atyerlcnv whn itcnb dlvrd ty prems.

In reply to your letter of 6 September, we are pleased to inform you that we can immediately supply the computer you require. Please let us know at your earliest convenience when it can be delivered to your premises.

*Refer to the ⅃ AgiliWriting · dictionary of STRINGS.